The Principal as Student Advocate

A Guide for Doing What's Best for All Students

M. Scott Norton
Larry K. Kelly
Anna R. Battle

Eye On Education
6 Depot Way West, Suite 106
Larchmont, NY 10538
(914) 833-0551
(914) 833-0761 fax
www.eyeoneducation.com

For information about permission to reproduce selections from this book,
write: Eye On Education, Permissions Dept., Suite 106, 6 Depot Way West,
Larchmont, NY 10538

Library of Congress Cataloging-in-Publication Data

Norton, M. Scott.
The principal as student advocate : a guide for doing what's best for all
students/by M. Scott Norton, Larry K. Kelly, and Anna Battle.
        p.   cm.
Includes bibliographical references.
ISBN 978-1-59667-189-8
1. Motivation in education.
2. School principals.
I. Kelly, Larry K., 1936–
II. Battle, Anna.
III. Title.
LB1065.N57 2011
371.2′012—dc22   2011013927

10 9 8 7 6 5 4 3 2 1

Sponsoring Editor: Robert Sickles
Production Editor: Lauren Beebe
Copyeditor: David Sassian
Designer and Compositor: Matthew Williams
Cover Designer: Knoll Gilbert

Also Available from Eye On Education

The Fearless School Leader: Making the Right Decisions
Cindy McCabe

Communicate and Motivate:
The School Leader's Guide to Effective Communication
Shelly Arneson

What Great Principals Do *Differently*:
Fifteen Things That Matter Most
Todd Whitaker

Principals Who Dare to Care
A. William Place

Leading School Change:
9 Strategies to Bring Everybody On Board
Todd Whitaker

Problem-Solving Tools and Tips for School Leaders
Cathie E. West

The Principalship from A to Z
Ronald Williamson & Barbara R. Blackburn

Transforming High Schools through Response to Intervention:
Lessons Learned and a Pathway Forward
Jeremy Koselak

Professional Development: What Works
Sally J. Zepeda

162 Keys to School Success:
Be the Best, Hire the Best, Train, Inspire, and Retain the Best
Franklin P. Schargel

Rigor in Your School: A Toolkit for Leaders
Ronald Williamson & Barbara R. Blackburn

Executive Skills for Busy School Leaders
Christopher Hitch & David C. Coley

Free Downloads

Many of the figures discussed and displayed in this book are also available on Eye On Education's website as Adobe Acrobat files. Permission has been granted to purchasers of this book to download these figures and print them.

You can access these downloads by visiting Eye On Education's website: **www.eyeoneducation.com**. From the home page, click on FREE, and then click on Supplemental Downloads. Alternatively, you can search or browse our website to find this book, and then click on "Log in to Access Supplemental Downloads."

Your book-buyer access code is **PSA-189-8**.

Index of Free Downloads

Figure 1.2 Traits & Behaviors of the Principal Student Advocate 18
Figure 2.4 (Name of School) Self-Reflection Exercise. 32
Figure 2.6 Principal's Building Blocks for an Inclusive School. 36
Figure 2.7 (Name of School) Statements of Fundamental Beliefs. 37
Figure 2.10 Student Behavioral Concern Referral. 43
Figure 2.11 Student Exit Statement 44
Figure 3.1 Student Services Commonly Available
       on School Campus 51
Figure 4.1 Organizational Characteristics Self-Analysis 79
Figure 4.2 Assessment of a Safe Environment. .92
Figure 5.1 Selected Student Disabilities and Services . . . . :97
Highlights (for sharing, review, and further study). . . . . .online only

Table of Contents

Free Downloads v

About the Authors xi

Acknowledgments xiii

Preface xv

1   The School Principal as Student Advocate: What It Means. 1

 Story of Clair 1

 Our Purposes 2

  Assessment of Your Student Advocacy Traits .2

 SAT Answers and Scoring Directions. 9

 An Explanation of the Answers to the SAT Assessment 10

 Summary of Traits and Behaviors of the Principal Student

  Advocate 16

 What Student Advocacy Is Not. 18

 Simulating Your Next Job Interview. 20

 A Look Ahead 22

 Summary. 23

 Application Exercises 24

2   Student Advocacy and the Inclusive School. .25

 A Time for Reflection 25

  Story of Cheryl 25

 Advocacy 27

 Determining Why Schools Exist: A First Step Toward Beginning

  an Inclusive School 30

 Defining an Inclusive School 33

 The Successful Principal and the Inclusive School. 35

 Effective Leadership of an Inclusive School 37

  The Importance of Vision. 38

  The Tool of Mental Imagery 38

  The Importance of Passion 39

 A Culture of Inclusiveness 39

 The Courage to Be an Advocate for All Students. 45

  A Case of Courage 46

 Summary. 46

 Application Exercises 48

3 The Principal as an Advocate for Student Services.................49
    A Principal's Thoughts..49
First Impressions Make a Big Difference 50
Shared Skills (Cross Training) 52
    Story of Juaneka: Making an Impression 52
Attendance Coordinator: A Role Much Greater Than Mere
    Accounting..53
Relevant Courses Support Student Achievement....................54
Relationships That Support Giftedness 54
Failure Is Not an Option......................................55
Family Focus for Advocating for Students 56
    Story of Mrs. Simpson: Advocacy Requires Both Time and
        Effort...57
Interventions Fostering Student Success 58
    Story of Mr. Karsten: The Results of Advocacy Are Not
        Always Immediate.......................................59
Guidance Services: Advocating for Student Success 60
    Story of Miss Howard: Stepping Into the Shoes of Students
        in Need..61
Rigor for All 62
    Story of Mr. Brown: Creating Opportunities for All Students 63
Expect the Unexpected 64
Community Social Services 65
    Story of Mrs. Hampton: Things Do Not Always Go Smoothly 65
Special Education and Students with Disabilities 66
    Story of Terrance: Advocacy Accentuates the Positive 66
Summary..68
Application Exercises 69

4 Creating an Environment for Teaching and Learning:
The Student Advocate's Primary Challenge 71
Creating an Environment for Teaching and Learning 71
Organizing Chaos: The First Day of School......................72
School Effectiveness: Creating a Desired Environment for
    Learning...73
    A Safe School Environment: A High Priority for the Principal 73
    A Safe School Environment: Creating a Family Atmosphere.......75
Constructing an Orderly School Environment 77
    Characteristics of an Organized School.......................77
    The Principal's Role in Creating an Orderly Environment.........79

Collaboration 80
Creating Opportunities Through Faculty Collaboration 82
Dealing with Disruptive Behavior in a Safe, Orderly Environment 82
Questions the Student Advocate Must Answer in
Disciplinary Cases. 85
Scenario 1 86
Scenario 2 87
Recommending Long-Term Suspension or Expulsion 88
Due Process for Students in Disciplinary Hearings 89
Advocate Role of the School Principal 89
Summary. 90
Application Exercises 91

5 **Principal Student Advocacy and the Student with Disabilities** 93
Let's Set the Stage, with You in the Lead Role 93
True or False? 95
Check Your Results. 95
How Far We Have Come as Advocates for Students with
Disabilities 96
The Many Special-Education Programs and Activities in Schools 96
Planning, Organizing, Implementing, and Evaluating Procedures. 98
1. Search and Find Procedures 98
2. Screening Procedures 98
3. Review-Team Procedures. 98
4. Implementation of the IEP. 99
Advocating for Special-Needs Students Through Policy
Implementation. 99
The Rehabilitation Act of 1973—Section 504. 100
The Education for All Handicapped Children Act of 1975. 101
Individuals with Disabilities Education Act (IDEA), Enacted
in 1990 101
How the School Principal Serves as Student Advocate in Special-
Education Programs 102
Advocates Support Special Education. 102
Advocates Practice Continuous Self-Development 103
Advocates Practice Collaboration. 103
How to Recognize a Principal Special Education Advocate 104
The Effective Principal Student Advocate and Competency-Based
Administration 105
Select Special-Education Competencies of School Principals 105

Snapshots of Student Advocacy in Practice. 108
The Student Advocacy Traits Post-Test 120
Summary. 120
Application Exercises 121

References. 123

About the Authors

Dr. M. Scott Norton is a former public school teacher, curriculum coordinator, associate superintendent, and superintendent of schools. He served as professor and vice-chairman of the Department of Educational Administration at the University of Nebraska–Lincoln and as professor and chairman of the Department of Educational Administration and Policy Studies at Arizona State University, where he presently is professor emeritus.

Dr. Norton is author and coauthor of college textbooks in the areas of human resources administration, the school superintendency, executive leadership and administrative management, and resource allocation. He has published articles in professional journals relating to teacher retention, teacher workload, organizational climate, employee assistance programs, the school principalship, competency performance, retaining quality school principals, and human resources administration.

He has received several national and state awards honoring his services and contributions to the field of educational administration. The American School Personnel Administrators Association, Arizona School Administrators, Inc., Arizona Educational Research Organization, and the University Council for Educational Administration are among the organizations that have recognized Dr. Norton for distinguished service to the field of educational administration.

He has held the positions of executive director of the Nebraska Association of School Administrators, president of the Arizona School Administrators Higher Education Division, Arizona School Administrators Board of Directors, treasurer of the University Council for Educational Administration, UCEA staff associate, regional representative for the National Association of Secondary School Principals, and other state and national offices.

Dr. Larry K. Kelly has served as a classroom teacher, assistant principal and principal, assistant superintendent, director of curriculum, and director of staff development in public schools. Other administrative experience includes the position of director of staff development for the Arizona School Administrators Association. In this role he directed the Arizona Administrative Assessment Center sponsored by the National Association of Secondary School Principals.

Dr. Kelly served as an adjunct professor for several years in the Department of Educational Administration and Supervision, Arizona State University, and continues to serve as a hearing officer for teacher and student cases in the Phoenix, Arizona area. In addition, he has served for thirty-five years as an NCA/CITA Accreditation team member and chair in Germany, Italy, Turkey, Japan, Egypt, and Saudi Arabia.

Dr. Kelly has authored or coauthored professional publications in the areas of resource allocation, the development of leadership through the school improvement process, and student self-scheduling.

He received the Excellence in Educational Leadership Award in 1996, and in 2007 he was inducted into the Mary Lou Fulton Education Hall of Fame at Arizona State University for his professional contributions to education in the state.

Dr. Anna R. Battle has served as a secondary school principal for eight years and as an assistant principal for five years. She teaches administration, leadership, and principalship courses for universities in Phoenix, Arizona. A collegiate athlete at Arizona State University and then a teacher of high-school students for twelve years and a coach for myriad school sports, Dr. Battle now teaches teachers and administrators effective strategies to improve academic performance of students in secondary schools.

Dr. Battle completed a bachelor of arts in the area of special education, K–12, a master of education in the area of secondary education, reading specialist and a doctorate of education in administration and supervision from Arizona State University. She has completed a Superintendent Certification at the University of Phoenix. Dr. Battle was honored by the National AdvancED Council for her leadership as a secondary school principal in 2010. She was named Arizona NASSP Principal of the Year in 2011.

Her professional affiliations include membership in these organizations: National Board of Certification for Athletic Trainers (Discipline), National Association of Secondary School Principals, and Arizona School Administrators Association (East Valley representative) and Arizona State Council (member for AdvancED/North Central Association).

Presently she serves as principal of Desert Vista High School in Phoenix, Arizona. Desert Vista High School has received considerable recognition as the best college-prep high school in Arizona. *U.S. News and World Report* honored Desert Valley High School as one of the top schools in the nation. She recently authored *Trust and Leadership* in (2010), which stresses the importance in schools of relationships among teachers, administrators, students, and parents.

Acknowledgments

The authors wish to acknowledge the many practicing school principals, assistant principals, other administrators, and teachers who participated in the interview sessions so crucial for the writing of this book. The majority of case studies, snapshots of student advocacy, and examples of best practices are based on the knowledge and experience of these educators. These participants contributed in a major way to bringing relevancy to the contentions and applications offered here.

Educational leaders collaborate with other important professionals with specific areas of expertise that support and enhance principals' abilities to advocate for students: special-education personnel, itinerant staff, guidance counselors, school psychologists, student-services staff, teachers on assignment, security staff, and those in community service agencies. We wish to acknowledge all of those who assist administrators in providing the best student advocacy practices in our schools.

We wish to express appreciation to all Eye On Education staff personnel for their contributions that were instrumental in the completion of the book.

Preface

This book is intended primarily for the actively serving school principal. Thus, it focuses on the principal's leadership role and the many responsibilities that come with the office, including several kinds of programs and activities that are specific to the administration of schools. However, teachers, other school administrators, and those who have aspirations of becoming a school principal may also find the information in this book of special interest.

In response to the many experiences encountered in the role, the school principal with some history of service most likely has given serious thought to his or her administrative philosophy and to the nature of the principal's professional relationships with faculty and students. In many instances, his or her formal education will not have included preparation in certain areas or provided adequate opportunity to consider the human, moral, and ethical dimensions that are always an aspect of the leader's decision-making responsibilities.

The practicing school principal comes to understand the paramount importance of serving as a decision maker and striving to carry out the moral responsibility of helping every student reach his or her full potential. This book provides the principal with practical ideas relative to answering the following questions: Am I truly doing what is in the best interests of each individual student? Am I truly an advocate when it comes to student rights? On what occasions, if any, have I stood tall against a policy or regulation that was not in the best interests of a student? What less dramatic, everyday behaviors exemplify student advocacy? What do I really believe and practice concerning such matters as student retention, student discipline, special student needs, and student inclusion in regular school classrooms and in extracurricular activities? What changes in my personal behavior might facilitate the accomplishment of my goals?

This book intends to challenge the practicing school principal to assess his or her present traits and behaviors relative to student advocacy, and to that end provides exercises for self-assessment. We provide a clear definition of student advocacy and of the behaviors, attitudes, and beliefs most commonly possessed by school administrators who truly are student advocates. We propose best practices relative to programs and activities that foster the interests of all students.

What is meant by student advocacy and what behaviors must be displayed and what strategies implemented to achieve it? What is an inclusive school? Student personnel services and special needs programs relate closely to student advocacy. How does student advocacy apply to all students? How is advocacy viewed as it applies to discipline? Why is the principal's advocacy so important in serving students with special needs? These are among the questions at the heart of this book.

We endeavor to provide the practitioner with tools and techniques that enable him or her to build a school culture that focuses on student advocacy. How the principal, as student advocate, might best work to build consensus among all school personnel is emphasized throughout. The principal is reminded of the importance of both the curricular and the co-curricular programs that are so vital to the needs, interests, and total development of each student. Such provisions include core academic offerings, the fine arts, athletics, technical programs, clubs, recreational activities, and programs that meet the special needs of students with disabilities.

Implicit in the book is a "calling" to help all students reach their full potential. We submit that as the school principal becomes increasingly effective in advocating for students, he or she is helping all students be more successful, both inside and outside the classroom.

1

The School Principal as Student Advocate: What It Means

Clair was an eleventh-grade student whose academic record was satisfactory in every subject. However, after completing the grade, Clair did not return to school the following fall for his final year and graduation. He was away from school for one entire year. When later asked why he didn't return to school, he simply said, "I was somewhat bored and just lost interest."

An assistant principal, who also served as an athletic coach, contacted Clair personally and encouraged him to return to school and graduate. The administrator indicated that he was available to help him arrange his class schedule and that the school needed him to participate in its football program. His encouragement was enough to motivate Clair to return to school, and his follow-up support helped Clair to graduate one year later. Clair was then drafted into the military service for two years, after which he entered the university and completed a bachelor of science degree in engineering. This enabled him to gain employment at the Sperry-Rand Corporation (later Honeywell International) in Phoenix, Arizona.

Initially, Clair was involved in resolving production problems for the autopilots on the B-52 bomber and the DC-8 commercial aircraft. Subsequently, he designed new autopilot components for the B-52 and the Boeing 727. Later he worked on spacecraft, managing the development of attitude controls for space vehicles. He also directed several NASA and USAF design programs, including the Galileo mission to Jupiter, the Gamma Ray Observatory, and the mission to Mars. Clair received three patents for gyroscopes, including one that was used on Galileo.

We cannot say what Clair's future might have been if one caring administrative student advocate had not taken the time and effort to support him at a crucial moment in his life. It is quite likely, however, that had he remained a high school drop-out, Clair's engineering contributions would have been lost to society and his personal self-respect and satisfaction diminished.

Clair's story dates from several decades ago, but it is similar to stories of student success in today's schools, thanks to the caring attitudes of principals who demonstrate the principles of a student advocacy on a daily basis.

Our Purposes

This book has several purposes. One is illustrated by the foregoing story: to improve the educational opportunities of all students, regardless of their present situation or academic standing. Efforts to ameliorate or resolve the problems of children and youth that inhibit them from pursuing educational opportunities can prevent drop-outs and mitigate behavioral problems. This goal entails the practice of advocating for and promoting every student's right to learn, with a clear intent to tie this learning to his or her real interests.

We accept the fact that you and other school principals do like students and want to see them succeed. But we ask you to consider these questions: Are you truly a student advocate? How does your administrative behavior demonstrate that you do, in fact, possess the traits of a practicing student advocate? Are you willing to assess your personal thinking and behavior relative to the many traits that principal student advocates possess? If so, we hope you will take the SAT (Student Advocacy Traits) assessment that follows. Read the directions carefully. In order for you to accurately determine your SAT status, you will need to respond to each of the fifteen situations from your personal perspective, and not according to what you think your supervisor would be looking for, what response would look good on an interview questionnaire, or what the rules require of you in your present role. You are the only one who will see the results, so be certain that they reflect what you truly believe and how you would behave relative to the matter at hand.

Assessment of Your Student Advocacy Traits (SAT)

Directions: For each of the following scenarios, check the response that is closest to *your personal disposition*. In each case, check the one action that best represents the behavior that you most likely would pursue. Don't be overly concerned that the situation might lie outside your current administrative responsibilities, rather focus on the matter at hand in view of your own beliefs. (Note: The validity of this assessment depends largely on whether or not your responses truly reflect *you* as a person—your thinking and your behavior.)

1. A second-grade student is reading below grade level and at the end of the school year has a reading achievement score of 1.2, a mathematics achievement score of 1.5, and an English proficiency achievement score of 1.4. Which of the actions below are you most likely to recommend?

_____ a. Promote the student to grade 3 with his or her peers, but with a recommendation that the student be given additional help by taking appropriate summer school instruction.

_____ b. Recommend attendance at summer school and then retesting to determine whether to pass or fail the student.

_____ c. Retain the student in grade 2 in an attempt to improve achievement scores.

2. A Boy-Scout knife is found in a third-grade student's desk. The student's teacher informs you that the student admitted bringing the knife to school. This is the student's first serious rules violation. Which of the actions below are you most likely to take?

_____ a. Suspend the student from school for the period stipulated in the school's student handbook; rules are rules.

_____ b. Meet with the student to determine why he brought the knife to school and then determine an activity for the student that would serve as a way to learn about the dangers of having things like knives in the hands of students.

_____ c. Dismiss the case, since this is the pupil's first serious disciplinary infraction.

3. A student at the departmentalized middle school of which you are principal is sent to your office for continuing failure to complete homework assignments for her English class. The teacher counts homework assignments toward 33 percent of the student's course grade. The school's handbook states that each teacher can assign one-half hour of homework each day. What action are you most likely to take?

_____ a. Determine why the student is not completing the homework assignments for the English class and assess the situation for other subjects that the student is taking.

_____ b. Arrange a meeting with the student and her parents to clarify the school's rules concerning homework and stress that the student is likely to fail if the assignments are not completed as required.

_____ c.   Set up an after-school study session with the student, in which
she is to receive help in completing the daily assignments.

4. Consider the last time that you wrote or participated in the writing
of an individualized educational plan (IEP) for a student. Which of the following is closest to your motivation for designing the plan?

_____ a.   The primary motivation was to please the child's parents and
gain their approval.

_____ b.   The primary motivation was to satisfy my supervisor or special-
education officials.

_____ c.   The primary motivation was to adhere to district/school policy.

_____ d.   The primary motivation was to adjust the workload of those
who were working with the student and to adjust budget
allocations.

_____ e.   None of the above. My fundamental motivation was to

_____.

5. A student in an English class is receiving marginal grades due primarily to low test scores. The student does well on multiple-choice and true/
false questions, but fails the essay sections of the tests. Which one of the following actions is closest to what you would do as school principal?

_____ a.   Be an advocate of the teacher's methods, not get involved in
matters of this kind, let the teacher do his or her job.

_____ b.   Recommend that the teacher design special tests for this student
that include only multiple-choice and true/false questions.

_____ c.   Underscore the fact that the student apparently knows the
material but does not seem able to get his or her ideas down on
paper. Ask about the possibility of giving the essay section of
the test orally to the student.

_____ d.   Give serious consideration to giving additional instruction to
the student in written English and essay writing.

6. Merton is a ninth-grade student in a middle school of grades 7–9. All
of his basic skills test scores are in the lower quartile for his grade. Merton is
a quiet student who seldom participates in class discussions, and teachers
tend not to call on him for verbal responses. Merton's only subject of personal
interest seems to be art. He also enjoys participation in athletics but has been
ineligible due to poor grades. One teacher commented to you that Merton is
just waiting until the end of the school year, when he can drop from school
and get a job, so as to obtain some spending money. Which action below is
closest to the action you would take in this situation at this time?

_____ a.   Plan a meeting with Merton's current teachers, physical education faculty, and the appropriate fine-arts personnel in the
school. Gain the ideas and recommendations of these persons

relative to how the school program can capitalize on Merton's special interests and talents in art and physical education. Ask Merton about his interest in pursuing the recommendations set forth by faculty personnel and solicit ideas from him relative to his personal interests at this time.

_____ b.   Ask Merton to come to your office after school. Be prepared to tell him about students whom you have known who have dropped from school before graduating and the many problems that they have faced in life thereafter. Point out clearly that his record reveals a similar destiny unless he wakes up and gets to work.

_____ c.   Do nothing in this case but support the teacher in any way possible. Be sure that she knows that you understand the problem facing her and that she and others in the school have done about all that they can to help Merton.

_____ d.   Refer Merton to the coordinator of work-study programs in the school district. This course could serve to provide Merton with a work skill with which he could earn some money and satisfy this apparent need.

7. You are walking the school halls when you notice one of the sophomore students standing by his locker crying. You approach him and ask, "What is the matter?" The student explains that his best friend was caught shoplifting in a downtown electronics shop and is being held by the police in the county juvenile detention center. Which behavior below is closest to the action that you would take at this time?

_____ a.   Let the boy know that this is what happens to those who do not obey society's rules of good behavior. Let him know his friend committed a crime and that this event should be a good lesson for both him and his friend.

_____ b.   Find out more about the boy's friend. Is he a student in the school? Are his parents aware of the violator's situation? Has the matter been reported to the appropriate office of the school district? What is his behavioral record in school?

_____ c.   Compliment the student for his caring attitude toward his friend. Refrain from belittling the friend or lecturing the student for associating with juvenile delinquents.

8. As school principal, you are called upon from time to time to substitute for an absent teacher who will not return for one week. As an English major, you often fill in for teachers in this subject area. On this occasion, the regular tenth-grade English teacher has assigned an essay for the class; students can write on one of two topics. One student approaches you in the

classroom and states that he is not interested in either one of the two topics suggested by the teacher and asks if he might write on another topic of special interest to him, that of the economic factors facing the nation's businesses at the present time. As the teacher in charge of the class at this time, which action below comes closest to your disposition on this matter?

_____ a. Explain that the student's request would be unfair to other students in the class.

_____ b. Point out that you are only a substitute and that the regular teacher has been fair in giving two options for topics to write about. Thus, he will be expected to comply with the regular teacher's assignment.

_____ c. Listen to the student's ideas relative to his topic of interest and provide any suggestions that you might have concerning his pursuit of the topic that he has in mind.

_____ d. Remind the student that there are many responsibilities in life that might not be of immediate personal interest. Tell him that pursuing areas of noninterest might lead to new avenues of interest for him.

9. The superintendent of schools asks you to come to his office to discuss a matter relating to a minority teacher in your school. At the meeting in the superintendent's office, he states that he is receiving complaints about the teacher from some parents, one of whom is a member of the school board. The superintendent asks that you give special supervision to this teacher and do whatever is needed to improve her teaching methods and address problems relating to her distinct Southern diction and pronunciation. Over the next few weeks, you work to establish rapport with the teacher and help her with lesson planning and appropriate teaching methods. The use of tape recordings to point out her rapid speech has proven effective in improving her communication skills. Improvement has been shown. In fact, you are of the opinion that the teacher is performing "above average" and will continue to improve. Students in her classes performed well on the last state achievement tests. A later call from the superintendent asks you to meet with him and the personnel director to discuss the teacher's situation. The superintendent opens the meeting with the statement that parent complaints have lessened but are still being received. He notes that the school-board member has asked about an executive session of the board on this personnel matter. The superintendent states that you should inform the teacher that she will not be asked to return next year and that she simply does not meet the professional requirements expected of permanent teachers in the school district. He notes that the teacher has the right to request a hearing on the matter. Which

of the following actions are closest to what you would do at this time at the meeting?

_____ a. Remain silent unless the superintendent asks for your thoughts on the matter.

_____ b. Agree with the superintendent that his decision seems best in view of the parents' apparent continuing concerns.

_____ c. Make it clear that you do not support the decision of non-renewal of the teacher and that you would have to appear in her support at any hearing that might be scheduled.

_____ d. Make it clear that if a hearing was to be held regarding this matter you would have to mention the fact of the teacher's improvement during the last several weeks.

_____ e. Tell the superintendent that you believe that such an announcement should come formally from the district office.

10. You are in attendance at a monthly "CCC" (communication, cooperation, and collaboration) meeting that is attended by representatives of the school board, the parents' organization, the school superintendent, and representative administrative and teacher personnel. A school-board member chairs the meeting. The major topic of discussion is the present policy on student retention in grade, which leaves student promotion decisions to the principal and staff of each school in the district. However, due to the state's current testing requirements and the fact that a few schools in the state have been "taken over" by the state for unsatisfactory progress, school boards have begun to view present practices as "social promotion" and are recommending that "it's time to get tough on student promotion." After an opening discussion of the matter, the chair of the CCC committee asks for recommendations. One school-board representative states, "Any student in the elementary grades who is achieving below his or her grade level in reading, mathematics, and science should be retained in the same grade the following year." Several persons in attendance agree with this suggestion. The chair asks if there is further discussion relative to the school-board member's recommendation. Which of the following actions is closest to what you would do at this point?

_____ a. Since I view this as a school-board matter, I would say nothing at this time.

_____ b. Since I mainly agree with the recommendation, I would stand and state this fact.

_____ c. Since I am fully aware and knowledgeable of the research on student retention in grade, I would stand and briefly relate the research in terms of the negative impact of retention on the welfare of grade-school pupils.

_____ d. Since I am not aware of any previous opportunity for all administrators and faculty or their representatives to discuss the matter of student retention, I would stand and ask that the suggestion be tabled until the administration and all concerned have had more time to study the matter.

_____ e. Since I oppose the recommendation philosophically, I would state the reasons for my opposition.

11. Which result or opportunity below do you believe would bring you the most enjoyment and satisfaction as a school principal?

_____ a. Being truly able to be an agent for change in the school.

_____ b. Witnessing a student's significant growth academically.

_____ c. Being recognized as the principal of a high-performance school.

_____ d. Being named the "school principal of the year" by the state administrators' association.

_____ e. Having one of your creative ideas concerning reading instruction adopted by the school district's curriculum committee.

12. Which of the following brief descriptions comes closest to your personal idea of what an ideal school would possess or look like?

_____ a. A school in which the goals set forth in its mission statement were truly a priority for all school personnel.

_____ b. A school in which the human and monetary resources were sufficient to support the mission of the school.

_____ c. A school whose mission statement makes it clear that the school administrators are the decision-making authority relative to matters of curriculum and instruction.

_____ d. A school whose mission statement makes it clear that curriculum and instructional decisions always are focused on the best interests and needs of its students.

13. When students say that they want their school principal to be fair, what do you think they mean?

_____ a. They want all students to be treated the same regarding disciplinary actions; the same "punishment" for the same violation.

_____ b. They want that decisions relative to discipline give them the benefit of the doubt.

_____ c. In disciplinary matters, they want the principal to hear their side of the story and to get the facts before acting.

_____ d. In disciplinary matters, they really are asking for a lesser "punishment" than they know is due in their case.

14. School principals often say that they became administrators because they always enjoyed their leadership roles in high school and college and wanted to make enough money to raise their family. Which thought or comment below comes closest to how you feel about such a rationale for becoming a school principal?

_____ a. The focus on leadership and security is close to my feelings in many ways.

_____ b. The statement is close to my thinking that the principalship does have many important responsibilities that require the individual's leadership.

_____ c. The comment lacks a focus on educational purpose.

_____ d. The comment lacks a focus on students as the primary consideration for school principals.

15. A student comes to your office and tells you that she feels sorry for the new teacher, Miss Smith, because kids are taking advantage of her kindness and lack of experience. The student says that some kids are making fun of her appearance and her inability to maintain order in the classroom. Which action below comes closest to your immediate response/behavior at this time?

_____ a. Tell the student that all first-year teachers experience similar problems and that the teacher will soon learn to handle these matters.

_____ b. Respond positively to the student's feelings for the teacher and caring for her in this situation.

_____ c. Thank the student for reporting this problem and indicate that you will follow-up appropriately on the matter.

_____ d. Set up a meeting immediately after school with Miss Smith and review the procedures for keeping order in the classroom. Remind her that she is the authority in the classroom and must be able to exercise this authority or learning cannot take place.

_____ e. Go to the teacher's classroom and observe the situation.

SAT Answers and Scoring Directions

The answers 1a, 2b, 3a, 4e, 5c, 6a, 7c, 8c, 9c, 10e, 11b, 12d, 13c, 14d, and 15b are most closely related to actions/behaviors of student advocates. Count the number of your correct entries and multiply this number by 6.6. This is your Student Advocacy Traits (SAT) score. (Example: 11 correct × 6.6 = 72.6. The score is 72.6, at the "Understanding" level in Figure 1.1 (page 10).

FIGURE 1.1 Student Advocacy Traits (SAT) Ratings

SAT Score	SAT Level	Level Defined/Evidence
100–90	Instructional	Extensive evidence of the school principal's grasp, at the total conceptual level, of student advocacy, and thus of the knowledge, skills, and ability to teach others about its practice.
89–80	Application	Noteworthy evidence of the principal's understanding of student advocacy and the ability to apply the concept in everyday practice.
79–70	Understanding	Substantial evidence of the principal's understanding of the concept of student advocacy and the ability to apply the concept in everyday practice.
69–60	Familiarity	Noticeable evidence of the school principal's knowledge of student advocacy and its utilization in everyday practice.
59–50	Initial	Some evidence of the principal's knowledge, skill, and ability to apply the concept of student advocacy in practice.
49–Below	Entry	Limited evidence of the principal's knowledge and understanding of the utilization of the student advocacy concept in practice.

An Explanation of the Answers to the SAT Assessment

Let's take a look at the answers to the SAT assessment and the reasons that the selected responses come closest to demonstrating the several traits or behaviors of a principal student advocate. The traits and behaviors of principal student advocates are illustrated in each of the preferred responses.

Response to Scenario 1: Response "a," promote the student to grade three, advocates best for the student, since it is in his or her best interests. Both empirical and research evidence have made it clear that students achieve more the following year when they are promoted with their peers, as opposed to being retained in grade. The principal student advocate is a leader who has a research posture centered on the best educational practices in such critical areas as student retention, student motivation, and the special needs of students. Response "c" cannot be supported in light of research findings concerning student achievement after retention, particularly as concerns the potential for the student to drop out from school altogether. (Failure in grade is among the primary contributors to student drop-outs. Failing twice is virtually a sure indicator that a student will be a drop out from school at some point.)

Response to Scenario 2: Response "b," meet with the student to determine why he brought the knife to school and then determine an activity for the student that would serve as a way to learn the dangers of having things like knives in the hands of students, best represents an advocate's response. Response "b" is a nonpunitive measure that encourages good behavior. Student advocates listen to the student and focus on ways to use a violation as a learning opportunity. The problem-solving approach to discipline offers a way to learn from mistakes and develops new attitudes and encourages personal responsibility for one's behavior. Responses "a" and "c" do not provide for positive student learning. Neither is in the best interests of the student.

Response to Scenario 3: Response "a," determine why the student is not completing the homework assignments for the English class and assess the situation for other subjects that the student is taking, reveals a caring attitude on the part of the principal advocate and gives consideration to the complexity of the dynamics that affect the performance and success of the learner. Attending to the reasons for not doing the work allows the principal advocate to place him- or herself in the shoes of the student and to examine possible causal factors from the student's point of view. Neither response "b" nor "c" represents a solution to the probable causes underlying the problem.

Response to Scenario 4: Response "e," none of the above, provided you an opportunity to offer a student-advocate answer. The primary purpose of an IEP is to program an educational pursuit that represents the special needs and interests of the student. This encompasses the student's academic, social, and physical needs. Response "e" supports student success. The other entries focus on the interests of other parties.

Response to Scenario 5: Response "c," underscore the fact that the student apparently knows the material but does not seem able to get his or her ideas down on paper, is an advocate's response. Asking about the possibility of giving the essay section of the test orally to the student reveals an understanding of the variables in learning styles and individualization. It centers directly on a solution for the underlying problem. As pointed out by Lavoie (2008), there is no one approach that is absolutely effective with every student: "If the child can't learn the way we teach, we need to teach the way he learns" (p. 7). Response "c" is also sensitive to the teacher's position, in asking about a possible solution rather than forcing an opinion on the matter. Response "a" is inappropriate because instruction is indeed an important responsibility of the school principal. Response "b" is less than satisfactory, since it eliminates opportunities for student self-expression. Response "d" would be a more long-range strategy, one that might be implemented in conjunction with the actions taken relative to response "c."

Response to Scenario 6: Response "a," plan a meeting with Merton's current teachers, physical education faculty, and appropriate arts personnel in the school, is the best advocate's response, since it has the potential of creating an environment for Merton in which he can focus on his personal interests and strengths and possibly preventing his dropping out of school. Is Merton or any other single student worth all this special attention? The student advocate looks out for and respects all students. The advocate tries to attain the best educational opportunities for each individual; such intentions are founded on respect for the student.

Response to Scenario 7: Response "c," compliment the student for his caring attitude toward his friend and refrain from belittling the friend or lecturing the student for associating with juvenile delinquents, shows the deepest appreciation of the individuality of the student. The student advocate is able to see things from the student's viewpoint, always keeping his or her best interests in mind. One trait of the student advocate is the ability to put oneself in the shoes of the other, trying to understand and appreciate the other's feelings and position. Responses "a" and "b" miss the point of student advocacy. The need in Scenario 7 is to deal with the student's feelings and the acknowledge his caring attitude.

Response to Scenario 8: Response "c," listen to the student's ideas relative to his topic of interest and provide any suggestions that you might have concerning his pursuit of the topic that he has in mind, is the response of a student advocate. It shows an understanding of the importance of creating an environment in which students can focus on their personal interests and strengths. The principal student advocate understands that there is no one method of learning for all students. Haberman (1995) makes an excellent point in this regard. He speaks of "gentle teaching" that attempts to eliminate discord in the classroom by focusing on learning rather than mere compliance. In Response "c," the school principal listens well, acts in the best interests of the student, and shows respect for his individuality. None of the other responses is student centered. For example, response "b" is more of a cop-out on the part of the school principal, one in which the principal is thinking more about him- or herself than the student.

Response to Scenario 9: Response "c," make it clear that you do not support the decision of nonretention of the teacher and that you would have to appear in her support at any hearing that might be scheduled, illustrates several important traits of principal student advocates, one of which is courage. An administrator cannot be a true student advocate unless he or she is committed to helping in matters related to questionable school policies and regulations, including teacher retention and fair and equitable treatment of staff. A principal student advocate is a leader who uses his or her influence and energy to protect students' interests, broadly conceived, including, of course, protecting valuable staff. Response "d" is considerably less courageous than response "c." You most likely have heard of school principals who have been released for taking stands opposite those of the school superintendent, the school board, or perhaps a community group. A student advocate is one whose commitments and beliefs relative to students are revealed in his or her actual behaviors and decisions about school policies, curriculum, student and staff relations, and related school programs. Thus, student advocacy frequently requires courageous stands on matters of policy and personnel.

Response to Scenario 10: Response "e," "Since I oppose the motion philosophically, I would state the reasons for my opposition at this point and time," is closest to that of a principal student advocate, revealing as it does an impulse toward direct action in opposition to school policies and regulations that he or she believes are contrary to the best interests of students. This courageous stand might place the principal in jeopardy with school-board members and perhaps with the school superintendent. Nevertheless, the true student advocate does not shy away from protecting the best interests of students at all times. The possibility of adopting school policies and regulations that are not in the best interests of students and that are not founded on the best research and evidence must be pointed out by the principal advocate, because such matters most often are beyond the reach of students themselves. A principal student advocate speaks for or on behalf of students. As an advocate, the principal protects the legal, civil, and human rights of students.

We understand that this prescription may be problematic for some teachers and administrators. Might we realistically expect an inexperienced principal to stand up and advocate contrary to the decision of the superintendent or school board? Perhaps not. Nor do we expect the teacher or principal to advocate in complete disregard of the policies and politics of schools or of other parties that oversee the schools. We discuss the need for good judgment and personal courage as related to advocacy elsewhere in this book. Although Response "c" has merit, it would not require the level of courage that would be shown in Response "e."

Response to Scenario 11: Response "b," witnessing a student's significant growth academically, reflects the kind of job satisfaction prized most by student advocates. Response "b" centers on gratification related to the growth of students. Each of the other responses, although associated with positive outcomes, is more related to satisfying the ego of the administrator. Principal student advocates gain most of their true professional enjoyment through witnessing student growth—academic, physical, and attitudinal. They take advantage of every opportunity to improve the learning experiences of students.

Response to Scenario 12: Response "d," a school whose mission statement made it clear that curriculum and instructional decisions always are focused on the best interests and needs of its students, best reflects the advocacy trait of student-centered behavior. You most likely would agree that each of the other four responses are positive and perhaps desirable and might even result in some benefit for students. However, the student advocate's first priority in all decisions related to curriculum and instruction is helping each student be the best possible. Research supports the contention that student-centered curriculum strategies promote healthy school climates. For example, a publication of Phi Delta Kappa (1973) identified the following program characteristics as those associated with open, positive school climates: opportunities for active learning, individualized performance expectations, varied learning environments, flexible curriculum and extracurricular activities, support and structure appropriate to the learner's maturity, rules cooperatively determined, and varied reward systems. We submit that these factors reflect the principles of student advocacy.

Response to Scenario 13: Response "c," in disciplinary matters, they want the principal to hear their side of the story and to get the facts before acting, reflects what is most commonly stated by students themselves in relation to fair treatment. A school's student handbook often undermines the possibility of treating each student as an individual, since it sets rules whereby in similar situations every student is treated the same. This violates the student-advocate trait of treating students as important individuals in their own rights and according to their own individual needs. It is difficult to address the special academic, social, and physical needs of individual students while applying the same disciplinary strategies to every student for similar disciplinary violations. The learning need differs among the violators in such cases. It would seem that the same "punishment" for the same violation promotes a punitive approach to discipline. Student advocates emphasize non-punitive, respectful approaches to discipline. The principal student advocate distinguishes the nonpunitive approach from permissiveness; the nonpunitive approach is based on helping students learn by helping them resolve their own problems, through examining what has happened and what might need to be done ensure that such behavior is not repeated. A primary difference between schools with healthy climates and those with unhealthy ones is that those with positive climates have an identifiable problem-solving capacity that is used to decide school matters, including student discipline (Norton, 2008). Nonpunitive approaches necessitate respecting the student and hearing his or her side of the story.

Response to Scenario 14: Response "d," the comment lacks a focus on students as a primary consideration for school principals, is student-centered and thus reflects the principal's commitment to students over against the satisfaction of his or her own personal desires. Student-advocate principals enter into their role primarily for what they can contribute to the personal development of students. Certainly school principals are human, in that their personal and family considerations are of importance. However, personal security, professional development, and the personal satisfactions of leadership are not the primary reasons that student advocates assume administrative roles. Rather, commitment to the personal interests and needs of each student is of paramount importance.

Response to Scenario 15: Response "b," respond positively to the student's feelings for the teacher and caring for her in this situation, demonstrates the student-advocacy trait of seeing things from the student's perspective, always keeping in mind what is best for students. In response "b" the school principal stands in the student's place and takes care to acknowledge the feelings of the student. Responses "a," "c," and "d" do not focus directly on the thoughts of the student or on providing her with legitimate feedback concerning her caring feelings and attitude.

Summary of the Traits and Behaviors of the Principal Student Advocate

You have seen in the foregoing scenarios that the principal student advocate possesses several special traits that ground his or her personal administrative philosophy. Let's examine once again the answers to the SAT assessment and extract the several traits and behaviors that are revealed in the responses.

The School Principal as Student Advocate:

- ◆ **Is student centered.** He or she is a principal who is committed to helping each student be his or her best, one whose beliefs relative to student advocacy are revealed in his or her actual behaviors and decisions about school policies, curriculum, and related school programs.

- ◆ **Makes decisions that are in the best interests of students.** The principal understands the complexity of the factors that affect the performance and success of a student and supports and defends decisions that are in the best interests of all students.

- ◆ **Represents the special needs of all students.** This trait encompasses academic, social, and physical needs. Student advocacy focuses on identifying students' educational needs and then taking proactive steps to gain maximum support for meeting those needs through educational policy and state and federal laws. Proactive measures often are met with resistance and criticism. Unpopular actions on the part of the student advocate may be viewed by colleagues and others as permissive, or as attempts to gain popularity with students. It takes courage to stand up for students and the principles of advocacy when others favor policies that are more popular with other parties.

- ◆ **Sees things from the student's perspective.** The student-advocate principal always keeps in mind what is best for the individual student. This trait will be reflected in principal's philosophy relative to such matters as student discipline.

- ◆ **Stands up for student rights and concerns.** The student-advocate principal treats students as important individuals in their own rights and according to their own individual needs. This trait requires that the principal be knowledgeable of the rights of students and the administrator's responsibilities under state and federal laws. The principal takes courageous stands on educational initiatives that are contrary to the best interests of students.

- ◆ **Creates an environment in which students can focus on their interests and strengths.** This advocacy trait requires attention to the inclusiveness of the school's programs, such that the curriculum and instructional methods support individualism. Principals are committed to the statement, "I will respect my students." The principal accepts each student, regardless of his or her status, for the personal contribution that he or she can make to the success of the school's goals and objectives and to his or her own growth and development. The advocate leader uses his or her influence and energy to protect students' rights and interests.

♦ **Views the school as an inclusive learning site.** Each student is given the opportunity to participate in the school's programs and learn, in the continuous effort to reach his or her potential.

♦ **Is a good listener.** The principal student advocate is genuinely interested in assisting a student in meeting his or her personal needs and interests. Listening to the student's side of the story, learning about the student's special interests and talents, knowing students by name, and using effective listening skills are of paramount importance to student advocates. The principal makes an effort to see things from the student's perspective and is sensitive to the student's feelings.

♦ **Has a research posture.** The principal student advocate is a consumer, distributor, and utilizer of the best research relative to such critical issues as student retention, student motivation, special needs programs, student learning, and others. The principal's philosophy relative to such matters rests on a fact-based approach supported by quality research and generally accepted best practices.

Figure 1.2 summarizes many of the traits and behaviors of principal student advocates that have been noted in this chapter, as well as others that will be examined further in later chapters.

There are other important principal student-advocacy traits that will be identified and discussed in later chapters of the book. Right now, however, take a few minutes to consider your SAT assessment results. Ask yourself the following questions and think momentarily about your answers.

♦ Which of the traits and behaviors listed in Figure 1.2 do you possess and to what extent are they operational in your everyday practice? Am I doing what is truly in the best interests of each individual student? Am I truly a student advocate when it comes to standing up for student rights? On what occasions, if any, have I advocated against a policy or regulation that was not in the best interests of a student or students?

FIGURE 1.2 Traits and Behaviors of the Principal Student Advocate

- The principal is a good listener.
- The principal supports a research posture.
- The principal's school is student-centered.
- The principal supports an inclusive school.
- The principal shows respect for all students.
- The principal views each student as important.
- The principal knows and enforces student rights.
- The principal courageously advocates for all students.
- The principal persuades others to commit to advocacy.
- The principal sees things from the student's viewpoint.
- The principal implements non-punitive discipline methods.
- The principal is committed to helping each student succeed.
- The principal understands students' special needs and interests.
- The principal stands up for positive school policies and regulations.
- The principal encourages faculty and staff to know and use the personal interests of students in determining learning methods.

- What changes in my personal behavior might facilitate improvement in my student advocacy?
- What battles facing me or the school today am I willing to fight in order to advance the best interests of the students I represent (relative to issues of, e.g., student retention, student discipline, student inclusion in school programs and activities)?
- On a scale of 1 to 10, and in view of what was learned in this chapter, how do you rate yourself presently as a principal student advocate?

What Student Advocacy Is Not

When attempting to define a concept such as student advocacy, sometimes it is helpful to specify what it is *not*. Figure 1.3 lists six characteristics that student advocacy does not prescribe. First and foremost, student advocacy is not permissiveness. We agree with Denton (2007), who points out that respecting students and helping them in ways that lead to their self-development and personal autonomy is *not* the same as permissiveness. Listening to a student's side of the story in an attempt to understand the underlying causes of a violation of a rule, rather than immediately invoking a requirement for suspension or using other punishment, for example, is a constructive attempt to resolve the problem so that it does not happen again.

FIGURE 1.3 What Student Advocacy Is *Not*

Student Advocacy Is Not
- ◆ Permissiveness
- ◆ Equivalent to mainstreaming
- ◆ Only directed toward students with disabilities
- ◆ The sole responsibility of the school principal
- ◆ Placing students in sole charge of their destinies
- ◆ The relinquishing of the principal's or teacher's responsibilities

Student advocacy is *not* only for students with disabilities, such as those who are handicapped mentally, physically or socially. Student advocacy is a comprehensive attitude toward all students in the school. The aim of student advocacy is to support every student toward the goal of a successful school experience by providing the most effective program of academic subjects, as well as extracurricular activities that serve each student's special needs and interests. As previously noted, Lavoie (2008) points out that "each child is an individual and must be viewed as such. There is no one, solitary program or approach that works effectively with all kids . . . even if they have the same diagnosis or label. If the child can't learn the way we teach, we need to teach the way he learns" (p. 7).

Student advocacy is *not* the relinquishing of the principal's or teacher's authority and responsibility. In fact, the implementation of the student-advocacy perspective most often increases the time commitment of professional personnel in some ways. However, finding solutions to problems or getting students on a positive track of engaged learning ultimately saves the time and effort that would be required by remedial programs.

"Student centered" does *not* mean that students are in sole charge of their destinies in school. On the contrary, it is the aim of student advocacy to see that every student is provided the support needed to learn effectively and to utilize their personal interests and talents in choosing the educational activities that best suits their goals. When students are engaged in the learning process that is meaningful and successful for them, many problems of discipline, absenteeism, and apathy are resolved. Nevertheless, students need to be held accountable for their own "poor choices" or "poor judgment." The principal advocate understands this but approaches discipline from the perspective of promoting student learning, as opposed to punishment as itself a solution.

Student advocacy is *not* synonymous with such practices as mainstreaming special-needs students who are mentally, emotionally, or physically handicapped. Rather, student advocates work for the most appropriate placement for individual special-needs students. Their placement in the regular classroom is often the best and least restrictive situation for them. In other instances, separate classrooms, special tutoring, or homebound or one-on-one instruction are most appropriate to their special needs. You might be asking yourself, "Yes, but what about the laws or school policies that require main-streaming?" Principal student advocates work within the laws of the land but advocate for students by working to change rules that work against their best interests; they conduct action research that is useful in supporting changes of school policies and regulations that are not student centered. Advocates promote student rights. This behavior is one way that advocates work to overcome the obstacles to the success of students. Your call for changes in faulty school policies and regulations might not be accepted immediately. Over time, however, your thoughts may be echoed by others and eventually accepted for implementation.

The rights of students as set forth in Section 504 of the Rehabilitation Act of 1973 and the Americans with Disabilities Act Amendments Act of 2008 (ADAAA) are reflected in the many programs and activities that are implemented in pupil services programs nationally. These provisions are discussed in depth in later chapters of this book. In short, Section 504 underscores the rights of a child with a disability to have a free, appropriate, public access to an education (FAPE).

Student advocacy is *not* the sole responsibility of the school principal. Teachers, counselors, health-education personnel, special-education provid-ers, department and grade chairs, and other staff must be active as student advocates for an effective program of student success. As you know as a school principal, the success of any program or function within the school depends largely on your leadership. Lavoie (2008) contends that the key to getting your staff to support and assist in the implementation of the student advocacy concept in the school is summed up in the word *persuasion*. You must show the staff the benefits of student advocacy; you must be prepared for contradictions and objections; you must be willing to be agreeable by making certain compromises and adjustments when necessary; you must admit mistakes or miscalculations; and you must be patient in receiving the commitment of all staff, since such change often is intimidating to others. Nevertheless, when student advocacy is team oriented and staff see how it results in positive outcomes for students, commitment is likely to follow.

Simulating Your Next Job Interview

The scenario: You have been the principal of Wymore Middle School for six years, and now you are interested in the principalship of a new high school that is opening next year in a neighboring school district. You have completed the required application forms and have been selected as one of the four finalists for the position. An interview has been scheduled.

After completing the necessary introductions and briefly reviewing the community setting of the new school that you would be heading, and after your education and experience have been reviewed, the chair of the search committee asks for questions from members of the search committee.

One member opens in this way: "There seems to be a variety of views regarding the mission of the school and education today. Differences relative to what should be taught, how it should be taught, and what programs should be emphasized are prevalent. Such differences appear to be common among teachers, administrators, the school board, parents, and, yes, the various federal and state agencies that set certain educational guidelines. My question is this: "What are your beliefs about education today and what might you emphasize in your personal draft of the school's mission statement?"

Now for your response: Assume that you are speaking to the search committee and take two or three minutes to write your response to the committee member's question. Although you are likely to accept the position if offered, do your best to avoid telling the committee members only what you think they want to hear. Again, state your true response. Also, do not attempt to avoid a direct response, in the manner of, for example, "Here is what I did in my present school." The purpose here is for you to reveal your perspectives on education today and your personal views concerning a viable school mission statement.

OK, time in; check your response: We conducted interviews with several practicing school principals who were identified as among their school district's leading student advocates by teachers, the personnel directors of the school district, the school superintendent, and other school personnel, such as a school counselor.

Take a moment to compare your response to the interview question with the responses given by these practicing principals:

◆ The school's mission must first and foremost be student-centered, in that all students are prized for the contributions they can make to the realization of school goals and student growth and development, as defined by Maslow's (1987) concept of self-actualization.

◆ The school's mission must be to create a climate that encourages a focus on the strengths and interests of each student as an individual.

◆ The school's mission must be to gain a thorough understanding of the student's educational needs and to advocate educational services that promote the student's success in school.

◆ The mission of the school must be to identify the needs and interests of children and youth and to use this knowledge as the foundation for decisions about school policies, curriculum, instruction, and student assessment.

◆ The educational mission of the school should be to provide every student with the knowledge and skills needed to become a productive member of society and to address life's problems and challenges.

◆ A successful school program for children and youth has a pleasant, supportive, and safe learning environment that fosters life-long learning and enhances both the cognitive and affective skills that students need to contribute positively to the community in which they live. The school's mission must support this contention.

◆ A meaningful school mission is one with an explicit commitment to inclusion, to the ensuring that all students are afforded their right to a quality educational program, despite their individual differences.

◆ Historically, U.S. presidents and other political leaders have emphasized the importance of education in sustaining a democratic society, giving each citizen a fair chance and unfettered start in life (Abraham Lincoln), and supporting a healthy free-enterprise system. This concept should be addressed in the mission statement of the school.

◆ The development of the school's mission is a collaborative activity whereby all stakeholders participate in open discussion of the beliefs, goals, and objectives that result in an inclusive vision for the school, one that takes account of all students.

You will note that each of the above responses gives precedence to students. If your written response included one or more of the ideas above, your student advocacy traits are showing. Responses that emphasize having a high-performance school, having a school that has a high level of parental support, or having a staff that expects a high level of student achievement in each subject area are positive, but do not necessarily reveal the goal of a student-centered school.

A Look Ahead

The purpose of this chapter has been to explain and clarify the meaning of student advocacy. One primary feature of a program of student advocacy, termed the *inclusive school*, is featured in Chapter 2. The chapter defines and describes an inclusive school and explains why successful school principals commonly are found in inclusive schools. In addition, best practices relative to student advocacy are described as seen through the eyes of principals at work. You will be asked whether you believe that you have the courage to confront the challenges and sometimes the criticism that principal student advocates must face. You will be challenged to think about your own present practices and their identification with student advocacy.

Chapter 3 centers on student services and emphasizes the principal student advocate's leadership role relative to this important function. Chapter 4 centers on the principal's responsibility for maintaining an orderly environment for teaching and learning and its relationship to student advocacy. We believe that you will find the information concerning the nature of student hearings and the advocate's role in this process of considerable value and interest. The final chapter emphasizes student advocacy in relation to the school's special-education program. After a brief look at the progress that has been made in special-education programs nationally, you will have an opportunity to assess your knowledge of select features of special education, briefly examine the programs and activities in special education, gain an understanding of how present legislation advocates for and supports special-education students, see how principal student advocates support special education, and examine your personal status relative to the competencies required of principal advocates of special education. Chapter 5 concludes with several examples of principal student advocates supporting special education in practice. We believe that your personal student advocacy level may increase substantially after reading and thinking through the material presented in the following chapters.

Summary

Clair's story set the stage for the discussion of the traits and behaviors of principal student advocates. In that story, Clair, a high-school drop-out was motivated by a student advocate to return to school and successfully complete graduation requirements. As a result, Clair went on to a highly successful and productive life in the field of engineering. We submit that similar challenges and opportunities to advocate for students are prevalent in our schools today.

You were able to assess your current status relative to student advocacy by taking the SAT (Student Advocacy Traits) assessment. Perhaps you were not satisfied with your SAT rating. Nevertheless, when you learned more about the concept of student advocacy, its meaning and its related traits and behaviors, you developed a new foundation for increasing your skills relative to this stance. If your score was at the Understanding level or above, you are most likely already realizing the positive outcomes of student advocacy. You can look forward to extending your skills by giving thought to the information set forth in the ensuing chapters.

This chapter has examined not only what student advocacy is but also what it is not. Student advocacy is indeed student centered, but it does not translate into permissiveness or sanction only policies appropriate for special-education students; all students are important in a school actively committed to student advocacy. Principal advocates have many traits in common, one of which is a healthy respect for all students.

Application Exercises

1. Take no more than fifteen minutes to examine one week in your calendar of meetings and events. Note the nature of each meeting, contact, conference, visitation, or telephone call. Briefly note in writing your involvement in the event and also its status or outcome. Answer these two questions relative to each event: (1) What student advocacy traits or behaviors did you demonstrate? and (2) What influence, if any, do you believe your advocacy had on the outcome? Remember that the event need not be one relating to an overwhelming problem or decision. Most every communication, contact, or decision provides opportunity for the advocate to make a positive difference. We bet you will want to pat yourself on the back after this fifteeen-minute assessment.

2. Now, we want to present a real challenge for you. Think about the primary strengths of one of your best teachers. Discuss these strengths with the teacher and ask what you might do to help him or her employ these strengths more effectively in the school programs. Although you might have suggestions relative to this question, listen carefully to the teacher's ideas on the matter. Then do whatever you can to help the teacher implement one or more of the ideas. Give thought to ways in which the teacher could apply the traits of student advocacy to foster positive outcomes. If you find this activity successful, you might meet with other teachers. Both principals and teachers tend to soar with their strengths.

2

Student Advocacy and the Inclusive School

A Time for Reflection

If you are like many of us, from time to time you pause after a busy day in the classroom or the office and ask yourself, "Why did I ever decide to become a teacher?" or "Why did I ever leave the classroom for this?" In answer to the first question, perhaps the most common answer teachers give is "I like kids." Others may point to their love for a subject area, such as history, literature, music, or art, and the opportunity to share that love and perhaps instill it in the hearts and minds of students. They may profess a sincere desire to serve the community by helping young people become good citizens or tell you how thoroughly they enjoy the process of teaching and witnessing the excitement of students learning. Some may allude to the freedoms afforded by the profession—the extended time to engage in further study or travel or other leisure activities during recess or vacation periods. You may have become a teacher because of the impact a former teacher had on your life. It is entirely possible that as a student, as you sat in the classroom one particularly memorable year, you found yourself thinking along these lines: "I really like Mr. _____ and he likes me. I really like this subject. I think I would like to be like Mr. _____ and do what he does. I think I'd like to be a teacher." And so, the course is charted.

STORY OF CHERYL

As a sophomore in high school in a small mining town in central Arizona, Cheryl enrolled in a typing class taught by Mrs. Parsons. Cheryl liked Mrs. Parsons as a person and as a teacher and Mrs. Parsons liked Cheryl. Cheryl saw in Mrs. Parsons someone who cared about her and who showed a sincere interest in her as a person as well as a student. Mrs. Parsons also recognized Cheryl's determination to do well in school. As a junior, Cheryl enrolled in Mrs. Parson's shorthand class, and the teacher quickly observed Cheryl's skill in, talent for, and ability to learn shorthand. She also learned from Cheryl's other teachers that she was an outstanding student. Cheryl continued with Mrs. Parsons for a second year of shorthand. As graduation drew near, Mrs. Parsons felt strongly that Cheryl should continue her education by enrolling in the state university ninety miles from her home. Cheryl, who lived with her mother and younger sister, believed that college was out of the question because of her mother's very limited income. Mrs. Parsons would not take no for an answer. She wrote letters, helped Cheryl submit applications for scholarships, and called friends she knew at the university. Mrs. Parsons appealed to the principal, Mr. Evans, to write on behalf of Cheryl. Mr. Evans, principal of a high school of several hundred students, took the time to advocate for Cheryl by writing letters of recommendation to a number of colleges and universities. Of course, by the time she was a senior, Cheryl so admired and respected Mrs. Parsons that she knew that, if she were ever able to get into college, she wanted to be a teacher—just like Mrs. Parsons.

Even after all of her own, Mrs. Parson's, and Mr. Evans' efforts, Cheryl still had doubts that she would ever be able to attend college. Near the close of the school year, Cheryl received the good news. She had received a full-tuition scholarship from the state university. However, there loomed all the other related college expenses—housing, books, food, clothing. Mrs. Parsons again came to the rescue by calling a person who worked at the university to inquire whether or not there were any employment opportunities. To her and Cheryl's great surprise, there were. Cheryl obtained employment, graduated in four years, became a business-education teacher just like Mrs. Parsons, and retired after thirty-two years in the classroom. This would never have happened without Mrs. Parsons. We believe there are students like Cheryl and teachers like Mrs. Parsons all over your campus. Mrs. Parsons was an extension of her principal.

Leaving the classroom for an administrative position poses a particular set of considerations—especially for one who has derived a great deal of satisfaction from teaching and the direct interaction with kids and who has been successful in the classroom. But perhaps the prospect of being responsible and accountable for all aspects of the school's operations is intriguing and seems challenging. Maybe you feel it is time to move on.

Perhaps, one day, your school principal stops by your classroom, praises you for being such a good teacher, and asks if you have ever thought about going into administration? "Hmm," you think, "that is an intriguing idea." On a later occasion, as you are picking up your mail in the office, the principal asks if you have a minute and invites you into his or her office and, after some small talk, asks if you have given any more thought to the question and then, in a more direct fashion, says, "You know, I really think you should give serious consideration to becoming an administrator." Over time and after additional course work, another certification, and perhaps endless interviews, you become "one." And, now, here you are—a school principal or assistant principal—an administrator.

And now, in some of your more nostalgic moments, you might feel that you miss the kids, the laughter, the excitement, the interaction with students in your own classroom. You may even have wondered if you were still making a difference in the lives of students or whether you were now perceived merely as a figurehead at the school, one who puts out fires, puts kids in detention, or just attends meetings.

We offer this book in answer to such questions. Our purpose is to encourage, stimulate, and support you—the principal or assistant principal—in your belief that you can make a difference; you can influence the life of each student; and that each student in your school is given opportunities to study, learn, and enjoy enriching experiences that will remain with him or her for life. As we maintained in Chapter 1, you can sharpen your student advocacy skills, you can expand your student advocacy team, you can increase your student advocacy influence, you can develop and implement more effective student advocacy strategies, and, by doing so, make a significant difference in the lives of all who experience your school.

Advocacy

The overall theme of this book is that you can improve your advocacy for all the students in your school—for each and every student in your school. We go a step beyond common conceptions and contend that advocacy should extend beyond just those students with disabilities. This is not to suggest, of course, that rich educational experiences in a least restrictive environment should be denied students with disabilities. On the contrary, we promote advocacy in its broadest sense and urge that you become an advocate for all the students who enter your school.

In Chapter 1, we touched on what student advocacy is *not*. In this chapter, we want to reemphasize what advocacy *is* and to elaborate more thoroughly on what it entails. To become an advocate for anything or anyone means to speak or write in favor of, argue for, or recommend, possibly in a public setting. An advocate is a person who speaks or writes in support or in defense of a person or cause. As you read through this book, you are asked to reflect on issues, problems, situations, and obstacles for which you have, in fact, advocated in the past. Perhaps some of these have already been resolved, and

FIGURE 2.1 Log of Issues and Resolutions

Individual Student		Individual Teacher		Student Group		Curricular		Buildings & Grounds	
Issue		Issue		Issue		Issue		Issue	
1. Sally requesting schedule change to Ms. Jones class		1. Wants Johnny X. removed from class		1. Group of students wants to form a dirt bike club		1. Group of teachers wants to continue a low-enrollment class		1. Girls' softball team needs its own practice/game diamond	
2. Second Issue		2. Second Issue		2. Second Issue		2. Second Issue		2. Second Issue	
Resolution		Resolution		Resolution		Resolution		Resolution	
1. Denied does not meet prerequisites		1. Referred to counselor		1. Referred to activities coordinator notice in bulletin seeking sponsor		1. Discussed with district personnel; considered combining classes		1. Met with coach and team; discussed budget implications	
2. Resolution		2. Resolution		2. Resolution		2. Resolution		2. Resolution	

you have enjoyed some satisfaction in the outcome. Take some time to recall these and how you facilitated their resolution. What was your role? Did you involve others? If so, in what ways? What were your strategies? What roadblocks appeared? How did you get around them? How did you feel once the issue was resolved?

We anticipate there will be other scenarios presented here, however, reminiscent of situations of your own that are still unresolved, and where perhaps the odds in some ways are stacked against you. Still, you are intent on developing a strategy and effecting a resolution, because in this way conditions at your school will improve or another student will have a greater chance for success.

You might consider at this point maintaining a list or log of the major issues, problems, or concerns at your school with which you, another staff member, a committee, or a team are currently dealing. Consider developing a grid such as the one shown in Figure 2.1, in which the issues or problems are categorized. Recording the resolution of the issue or the action taken may prove useful in the future in identifying more frequently occurring problems or issues and developing ways to prevent their recurrence. This procedure enables you to create a database of problems or issues that, if there seems to be an inordinate number in one or two areas, might suggest avenues for research and may assist you and or your staff in determining priorities.

One of the strategies for enhancing your effectiveness as an advocate for all students in your school is to ask, prior to any decision being made, "In what way will my or our decision benefit students?" Although all decisions made at the school will have some impact on students, some will have a much greater direct impact than others. The greater or more direct the impact on students, the greater the consideration given to the question and the decision.

We once worked with a principal who was a member of Rotary International. In his office, the principal had posted the Rotary Four-Way Test. Often, as we were meeting in his office and about to arrive at a decision, he would point to the Four-Way Test and ask us to answer its questions (Figure 2.2).

FIGURE 2.2 Rotary Four-Way Test

Will it be BENEFICIAL to all concerned?

Will it build GOODWILL and BETTER FRIENDSHIPS?

Is it FAIR to all concerned?

Is it the TRUTH?

Are there similar questions your staff could develop that would be applicable to decisions being made on your campus? We suggest the school four-way test shown in Figure 2.3.

FIGURE 2.3 (Name of School) Four-Way Test

1. In what ways will this decision affect this student?
2. In what ways will this decision affect other students?
3. In what ways will this decision detract or take away from other programs?
4. (You develop the fourth question.)
5. (You develop the next question.)

As you and your staff embark on this journey of advocating for all students, and in so doing creating an inclusive school, perhaps you can identify additional questions that should be addressed at decision-making time.

Becoming an advocate means making a commitment to taking a risk, going out on a limb, exhibiting courage—to the point, perhaps, of becoming unpopular with those who take a point of view different from yours. But you have made the decision to *advocate* for that student, issue, or cause and are willing to take that chance.

Determining Why Schools Exist: A First Step Toward Becoming an Inclusive School

At the beginning of this chapter, we asked you to recall two questions that you had likely asked yourself at one time or another: "Why did I ever decide to become a teacher?" and "Why did I ever leave the classroom for this?" Now we are asking you to carefully consider two additional questions, only this time we are asking that you pose the questions to your faculty and staff. For those of you who have already answered the questions, this activity can serve as a reminder and reinforcement of what you and your staff have already affirmed.

First, we suggest you to deal with the "purpose" question: "Why does our school exist?" or "What is our purpose?" or "What is our reason for being here?" Later, in this chapter and in Chapter 4, we explicitly address the mission of the school. At this point, however, we suggest that you deal with the "purpose" question first. We suggest that there is a subtle difference between "purpose" and "mission." We take the position that the purpose of the school concerns the "student reasons" for its existence. Schools exist because of and for their students. If it were not for students, schools would not exist. The school's mission, on the other hand, is more concerned with how the school goes about satisfying its purpose. Therefore, we feel it is important for you and your staff to discuss, internalize, and institutionalize the "student reasons" for your existence first. Our second question deals with those fundamental characteristics that describe your school: "What do we stand for?" or "What one-word descriptors best characterize our school?" Before engaging in that exercise, however, let's take a step back in time and reflect on how schooling in America began.

The first school in America was the Boston Latin School, founded on April 23, 1635, in Boston, Massachusetts, on the belief that the only good things are the goods of the soul. School was held in the home of the headmaster, which suggests that enrollment was quite small. Contrast this with enrollment in public elementary and secondary schools today. According to the US Department of Education, National Center for Education Statistics (2010), 88,214 public elementary and secondary schools were operating in the United States in 2009–2010. Some of these, of course, are specialized, such as magnet schools or special-interest or special-needs schools. Why so many schools, and why do they exist? One might argue that schools exist for the community, state, or nation, to equip its citizenry with the knowledge, skills, and experiences that will ensure a stronger, better prepared, and globally competitive workforce. Certainly the reason or reasons schools exist today are far more complex than those in 1635. Purely and simply, we would argue that schools exist today for the student—that your school exists for its students—both individually and collectively. But perhaps you should probe more deeply or review more thoroughly some important questions dealing with the "whys" of your school. For starters, we suggest that you answer the four questions in Figure 2.4 (page 32). We urge you to give serious thought to your answers. We suggest that you then pose the same questions to your faculty, in small group sessions, allowing plenty of time for reflection and discussion.

We believe that if you and your entire staff have carefully and thoughtfully answered the "why" questions and are fully committed to the notion that schools exist for all students—again, both individually and collectively— then your school has taken a major step toward becoming an inclusive school.

Our second question, "What do we stand for?" must also be addressed. Answering it also calls for serious soul-searching on the part of both you and your staff. Answering it will take time and dedication and usually more than just one faculty or committee meeting. Investment in the process, however,

FIGURE 2.4 (Name of School) Self-Reflection Exercise

Question	Answer
Why does our school exist?	
Why are we (teachers & staff) here at this school?	
What is our purpose for doing what we are doing?	
For whom do we exist?	

offers the opportunity of a bonding, collegial experience for faculty and staff, one that generates a cohesiveness that will yield satisfying returns for your school.

What your school stands for is a reflection of the school's purpose. What your school stands for reflects the basic principles, values, and beliefs that shape and guide decisions, the ways in which all persons interact, and the way you, your faculty, and staff perceive each student that enters your campus. For example, Loyola University Maryland's value statement clearly states that the university's core values include academic excellence, Jesuit heritage, sustainability, and community service. On its website, the Container Store, based in Dallas, Texas, clearly states: "Not only was The Container Store built on great products, but it was structured around some very basic and fundamental values and business philosophies about treating employees, customers and vendors with respect and dignity—we call them our Foundation Principles." In a discussion with employees, Steve Jobs, CEO and cofounder of Apple, clarified Apple's approach to marketing by emphasizing what Apple stands for: "What we're about isn't making boxes for people to get their jobs done. . . . Apple's about something more than that. . . . we believe that people with a passion can change the world for the better." He went on to articulate that Apple's emphasis in the future will be to honor people who have changed the world.

Jobs cited Nike as an example of honoring people rather than emphasizing product in advertising and marketing, pointing out that Nike advertisements rarely focus on the superiority of its product relative to those of its competitors. Rather, Nike advertisements focus on great athletes—on people and their performance. Nike's ads focus on the person and what the person has accomplished while using its products. We should acknowledge that, even in these most trying of economic times, these are organizations—Apple, Nike, the Container Company—that continue to flourish, and they are organizations that have a clear sense of purpose that is a continuing focus. The lesson for school administrators—for you the principal—is that your school will enjoy even greater success when you lead your faculty and staff in the process of identifying and committing to a set of core values and beliefs that will guide your decisions and relationships in the days, weeks, and years to come.

Defining an Inclusive School

We are advocating inclusiveness in the broadest sense of the term. The inclusive school movement had its beginning in the late eighties and early nineties. There were two schools of thought during these years. The Regular Education Initiative (REI) was a concept advanced by former assistant secretary of education Madeleine Will. The goal of the REI was to merge special-education and regular schools into a single system. A similar school of thought, called Inclusion, was based on the belief in a return to one educational system for all students and an instructional program for every student that meets his or her individual needs and learning characteristics.

In keeping with the philosophy of inclusion, schools should commit to a number of basic principles: (1) the culture of the school is one where every individual is shown value and respect; (2) there is an ethos of learning and achievement where learning is supported, recognized, and celebrated; (3) everyone is able to make a positive contribution; and (4) every student feels welcome and has a strong sense of belonging.

In essence, the inclusive school movement evolved from a strongly felt need to include students with disabilities in general-education classrooms. The result was the passage of legislation that provided the impetus for placing students in a least restrictive environment, which for many students with disabilities meant a general-education classroom. We agree with and strongly support the notion that each student should enjoy an educational experience that maximizes his or her options for learning, which means placement in classrooms that facilitate that experience. This concept is discussed further in Chapters 3 and 5.

We contended previously that an inclusive school be described as one where all children, including those with diverse abilities, needs, talents, interests, goals, backgrounds, ethnicities, and motivations, can learn and come to school wanting to learn. As President John F. Kennedy stated in a civil-rights address delivered in 1963, "Not every child has an equal talent or an equal ability or equal motivation. But they should have the equal right to develop their talent and their ability and their motivation" (cited in Ravitch, 1985, p. 141). An inclusive school enables each child to develop his or her talents and abilities and to realize his or her hopes and dreams. Just think of all the students entering your school today and the innumerable experiences, expectations, talents, interests, and desires they bring. It is our duty to provide the services, experiences, support, and care that will allow them to do just what President Kennedy so clearly stated was their right—"to develop their talent, their ability, and their motivation."

Every student entering your school has an interest, gift, talent, or degree of motivation concerning something. Nowadays, that interest may be in music, art, science, insects, video games, tattoos, soccer, drawing, or one of the thousand other things competing for his or her attention. Whenever the student is exposed to that special area of interest, something inside is sparked. A connection is made with the item or experience and the student becomes engaged by, even excited about, the experience. Consider a metaphor: nestled in the mind of that student is a toggle switch. In electronics, a toggle switch is a component that completes or breaks an electrical circuit. When the switch is "clicked on" the circuit is completed and electricity flows, and when the switch is "clicked off" the circuit is broken and current no longer flows. Consider visualizing every student entering your school having at least one "toggle switch" imbedded in his or her mind. Some students may have many switches depending on their talents, interests, needs, and desires. When a student walks onto your campus, is the recipient of your "hello," your smile, your pat on the back, and then enters a teacher's classroom, consider that any one of you may very well be the one who "flips the switch" in that student's mind that connects him or her with school and creates a current and a climate for success that may well circulate throughout the school—success breeding success.

The teacher, administrator, coach, or staff person who flips on the toggle switch in a student's mind and connects him or her to a particular area of interest may very well help create that master connection that channels energy into all other areas of his or her schooling (see Figure 2.5).

Inclusion, in its broadest sense, must take into account all the stakeholders of the school, including—besides students—faculty, staff, parents, neighborhood residents, and community and business organizations. The principal

FIGURE 2.5 Connections

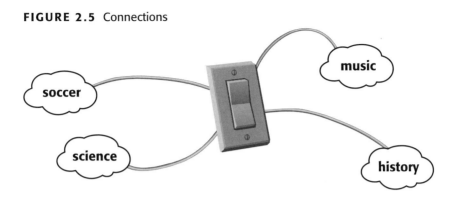

who perceives inclusion as the process of welcoming all students who enter his or her school and then orchestrating the contributions of all stakeholders into a well-organized, efficiently functioning system of providing the experiences, interactions, and challenges that will enable each student to achieve his or her goals and dreams and become a well-educated and prepared citizen—that principal carries the vision of an inclusive school in the most comprehensive sense. A school that overlooks the special interests and needs of a student cannot be considered as a totally inclusive school.

The Successful Principal and the Inclusive School

Success as the principal of an inclusive school entails a number of fundamental components, as shown in Figure 2.6 (page 36). These are incorporated into his or her life at school on a daily basis. The principal is constantly on alert that the components are in place, are functioning smoothly and efficiently, and that each member of the school team is continually reminded of the importance of each component and how it relates to the school becoming inclusive.

Creating a fully inclusive school begins with the principal—purely and simply. As noted in Chapter 1, the principal must possess and demonstrate a number of critical beliefs, characteristics, traits, and behaviors. These include:

- ◆ being student centered, making decisions that are in the best interests of students
- ◆ representing the special needs of all students, seeing things from the student's perspective
- ◆ standing up for student rights and concerns

FIGURE 2.6 Principal's Building Blocks for an Inclusive School

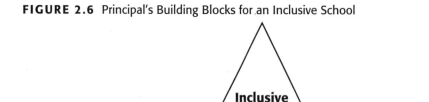

- ◆ creating an environment in which students can focus on their interests and strengths
- ◆ viewing the school as an inclusive learning site
- ◆ being a good listener
- ◆ demonstrating a research posture

Indeed if the principal is the key to creating an all-inclusive school, then we must discuss the most basic aspect of the principal's administration of the school—his or her fundamental beliefs. Effective leadership emanates from his or her basic, fundamental beliefs and convictions about students and schooling. The principal of the inclusive school will commit to a few basic beliefs. We hope that, in time, you and your staff will identify and internalize additional fundamental beliefs that are applicable to your school and situation. So, let us begin with four basic beliefs for your consideration.

First, the successful principal of an inclusive school must believe that each and every student *can and will* learn in his or her school. Second, the successful principal of an inclusive school must believe that his or her school has the tools to enable each and every student to learn. Third, the successful principal of an inclusive school must believe that his or her school faculty and staff are predisposed to ensure each and every student can and will learn in his or her school. Finally, the successful principal of an inclusive school must believe that he or she has the ability, leadership skills, energy, and enthusiasm

FIGURE 2.7 (Name of School) Statement of Fundamental Beliefs

Belief About . . .	*Statement*
Students	
Schooling	
How the school should serve students	
How the curriculum should serve students	

to create a culture of inclusiveness that will motivate and empower staff to enable each and every student to achieve at the highest level.

Not all children enter your school with the same level of motivation or readiness for learning. Your commitment to establishing a positive climate for learning, providing strong teacher support, encouraging a collegial relationship between faculty and staff, equipping your school with the necessary resources, and advocating for strong parental engagement is essential for ensuring that every child in your school will learn and succeed. To internalize and institutionalize these commitments, the school principal must meet with the staff and identify basic beliefs about the school, its students, and schooling and then collectively write statements of each, statements with which all agree and to which all will be committed. Using the format suggested in Figure 2.7, complete statements for each belief.

Of course, we suggest that you and your staff expand the number of critical beliefs and then develop statements for each that will guide, motivate, and enable you and your staff to achieve the desired result—a comprehensively inclusive school.

Effective Leadership of an Inclusive School

The principal is the key person, the catalyst, the spirit behind an inclusive school. The principal sets the tone for all personal interactions—for faculty and staff with each other and with students and for students with each other and with their teachers and the support staff. We have already discussed the principal's fundamental beliefs and behaviors and their impact on his or her leadership. Because you want your school to be inclusive, you must persuade your faculty, your staff, and parents that the school's becoming inclusive will serve all students in the best possible way, in terms of successfully preparing them for the future.

The Importance of Vision

It is critical that the principal have a clear picture or image of the school as an inclusive school in the most comprehensive sense. As Bennis (1989) wrote in his best-selling *On Becoming a Leader*, "The first basic ingredient of leadership is a guiding vision. The leader has a clear idea of what he wants to do . . . and the strength to persist in the face of setbacks, even failures" (p. 39). The principal's vision is shared with faculty, staff, and stakeholders, and they are given the opportunity to further shape it and give it its final, collaborative form. Only then will a complete understanding of and commitment to the vision be achieved. The vision becomes the target toward which the strategic movement of the school will aim. Faculty, staff, and stakeholders will say, "This is where we want to go and what we want to become."

The Tool of Mental Imagery

A vision may very well begin in the form of a mental image. Mental imagery is a powerful tool in preparing and equipping an individual for success—provided the image is a positive one. This has been demonstrated repeatedly in, for example, athletics, dance, even public speaking—the effectiveness of first visualizing the desired result, before setting about to prepare, train, and, finally, execute.

Mental imagery is used in sports to enable the athlete to achieve at his or her highest level. Achievement at the highest level should be the goal for our students as well as for ourselves and our schools. Find a comfortable and quiet place, take a relaxed position, close your eyes, and develop a mental image of yours as an inclusive school. Once that image has been formulated, you should give it written form, in a short paragraph. Commit it to memory. Now, whenever you get the opportunity, you share that vision with anyone on your campus who will listen, you incorporate it into school improvement meetings and site-council meetings, and you share it with your student leadership. In other words, your vision of your school becomes embedded in your conversation, whenever you speak as a principal and with whomever you interact.

The Importance of Passion

Another basic ingredient of leadership identified by Bennis (1989) is an "under-lying passion for the promises of life, combined with a very particular passion for a vocation, a profession, a course of action" (p. 40). The successful principal student advocate in an inclusive school will be passionate in pursuing his or her vision of what the school can and will become. Bennis goes on to say, "The leader who communicates passion gives hope and inspiration to other people" (p. 40). The principal's commitment to ensuring that no student "slips through the cracks" or is "left behind" during his or her time at the school will inspire others on the staff to make sure that quiet Johnny or withdrawn Susie are reached and challenged and successful. Think about an issue, problem, cause, or student in a difficult circumstance that you have been passionate about—would be willing to go to the mat for—the one that awakens you in the middle of the night or occupies your thoughts off and on throughout the day. Develop a plan, a course of action, to resolve the problem and then implement it.

A Culture of Inclusiveness

Once you have developed and passionately articulated your vision, as the successful principal of an inclusive school you can create a culture of inclu-siveness by (1) involving students, staff members, and parents in the decisions made by or on behalf of the school, (2) building, enabling, and empowering teams in the school and, (3) fostering a spirit of openness and collaboration throughout the campus.

We begin with involvement—making sure that all parties with an inter-est in the success of the school are represented in its operation. On becom-ing governor of Texas George W. Bush (1999) wrote, "The first challenge of leadership . . . is to outline a clear vision and agenda. The next challenge was to build a strong team of effective people to implement my agenda" (p. 97). After developing your vision, presenting it to the faculty, staff, and stake-holders and giving them the opportunity to further shape it, your next task is to form your leadership team. The challenge is to identify the parties that have a vested interest in your—now their—school. These will include faculty, staff, students, and parents. Most principals have a core group of advisors, such as the administrative team or the "principal's kitchen cabinet." Grade-level chairs or academic-department chairs may also constitute this group. In either case, it is with this group that the principal will likely initiate discus-sion of the most sensitive or critical issues facing the school before introduc-ing the matter to a wider audience.

One may also consider local businesses, those within the attendance boundaries of the school, as well as service clubs or community groups. Another possibility is the "neighbors" of the school—those who live in close proximity and whose homes students pass on their way to and from school. These individuals might easily be involved as "observers" looking out for individuals who are not students or parents and who may represent a danger to the safety or welfare of students.

The question of how you are going to involve such groups in the the day-to-day business of the school is important. A major consideration is the extent and frequency of each group's contributions, direct or indirect, to school operations. For example, some groups—teachers and staff members—contribute by the minute. Some, such as site councils or parent-teacher associations, contribute on a weekly or monthly basis. Those individuals or groups that make more frequent and direct contributions will, of course, be the ones with which you meet more frequently. These groups represent the more specialized groups or "teams" that you and your school leadership team have identified and formed.

Given the size of most schools today, it may be very difficult or impossible for the principal to personally engage himself or herself with the aspirations, plans, activities, and experiences of each student. Because of this reality, we liken the role of the principal to that of the coach, let's say, of a professional football team. Like the football coach, the principal must coordinate the activities of all the professionals, those on offense as well as those on defense.

First, the team has one objective—to win games. In order to win games, the team must both score points and prevent the other team from scoring more points than it does. In order to score, the team has to move the ball down the field and have one player cross the goal line and score a touchdown or get close enough to kick a field goal.

Second, the coach must coordinate the efforts of at least eleven players if the team is to score. Additionally, the coach must put eleven players on the field who will prevent the other team from scoring. To do this, the coach must select from over fifty professionally trained, highly skilled, and highly motivated players the eleven best for offense and the eleven best for defense. (See Figure 2.8.)

There are eleven different positions on offense and seven on defense. The skills requirements for each position are different, as are those for speed and size. The successful coach reiterates constantly that the mission of the offense is to score points and the mission of the defense is to prevent the other team from scoring points. Ultimately, it is up to the individual player to exert his best effort if the team is to accomplish its overall objective. You might ask, "How does this relate to the school principal?" The role of the school principal very much parallels that of the coach. Consider the following.

FIGURE 2.8 Typical Football Positions

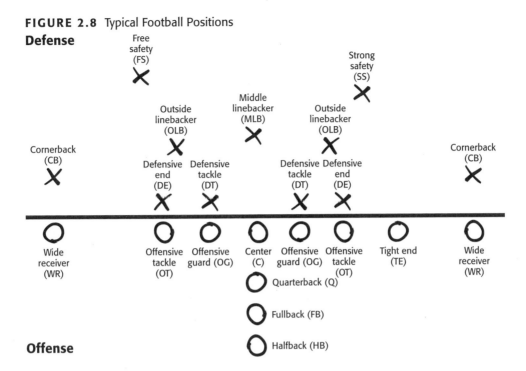

First, every school has a mission which, in simplified terms, boils down to enabling students to achieve and succeed in whatever endeavors they attempt. Jones and Kahaner (1995) stated in their book *Say It and Live It, The 50 Corporate Mission Statements That Hit the Mark,* "Corporate mission statements . . . are the operational, ethical, and financial guiding lights of companies. They are not simply mottoes or slogans; they articulate the goals, dreams, behaviors, cultures, and strategies of companies more than any other document" (p. ix). One might say that the principal's role is to always keep the faculty motivated and their efforts maximized toward achieving this mission. When the defensive unit is on the field in a football game, its mission is to prevent the other team from scoring. You hear the fans yelling loudly from the stands, "Defense . . . Defense . . . Defense." When the offensive unit is on the field, the chant is "Go . . . Go . . . Go." The coach may be walking rapidly along the sidelines pumping his fist, encouraging whatever unit is on the field to reach beyond what they thought possible to achieve the goal. The principal is visible in the classrooms or on the playground encouraging, supporting, standing behind teachers. He or she is out on the playground or on the diamond or in the gym pumping a fist, encouraging athletes to exert their best efforts. He or she will be at school concerts or plays applauding a fine performance. In short, the principal is the faculty, staff, and students' greatest cheerleader as well as their coach.

Second, every campus has a faculty with a wide variety of talents and an extensive knowledge of and preparation in teaching skills, subject content, and understanding of learning styles and behaviors. As coach, you work with your faculty and staff to effectively maximize and utilize their talents, skills, and interests. Your entire faculty and staff have become your team, and you work to assist them in more clearly understanding their role on the team, to motivate them to commit to that role, and to create a state of readiness so that when the situation requires, each team is ready to spring into action. There are, very broadly speaking, two types of teams in your school—academic and nonacademic. Figure 2.9 presents one such division of school personnel.

FIGURE 2.9 School Team Categories

Academic Teams	*Nonacademic Teams*
Grade Levels/Professional Learning Communities	Pupil Personnel Services
Subject Matter Disciplines	Athletics
Performing Arts	Clubs
Media	Special Interest Groups

The academic components are comprised of the certified teachers on your faculty—grade-level teachers in elementary schools and subject matter specialists in middle, junior high, and high schools. All students are placed in the appropriate academic setting based on their academic achievement, grade level, or special needs. For students new to the school, information pertaining to placement is obtained during the registration process and the student is assigned to the most appropriate classes. For continuing students, placement is based on the student's history in the school. There are some students who may be barely hanging on, who show no interest in school, or who begin to display problematic behaviors such as truancy, gang affiliation, or withdrawal. For the elementary school teacher, who commonly is with the student throughout the school day, such changes in behavior may be relatively easily recognizable. For the middle school or high school teacher who may see the

FIGURE 2.10 Student Behavioral Concern Referral

> ### ABC School
> *Student Behavioral Concern Referral*
>
> Name of Student: _____   Number: _____
>
> Referred to: _____   Date: _____
>
> Nature/type of behavior observed: _____
>
> _____
>
> _____
>
> _____
>
> _____
>
> Referred by: _____   Position: _____

student only one class period per day, the changes may not be so noticeable. Once the behavioral changes are observed, however, the "advocacy process" can be activated—provided, that is, the school has a process by which, when questionable and sustained changes in the behavior of a student are noted, a staff member is notified and follow-up procedures are activated. If not, then a process needs to be developed, steps by which it is activated defined, faculty and staff trained in its implementation, and a record-keeping system created. The school may want to consider a half-page form such as that shown in Figure 2.10. It should be noted that the form is *not a disciplinary referral*. It is a "referral of concern." Such a form is submitted by a concerned staff member to a person such as a counselor or a team that can most appropriately deal with the student and the issue.

Already, the principal, as coach, has identified those special skills, talents, and abilities possessed by the faculty and staff. In addition, the principal has already put in place special services and resources—academic teams and nonacademic teams—designed to address the needs or problems emerging through behaviors of those students losing their "connection" with school. Now it's time to call your teams into action in order to take additional preventive or corrective action concerning the student.

Why has the concept of team been incorporated into our discussion? Perhaps you have seen the motivational poster carrying this slogan: "TEAM, Together Everyone Achieves More." We strongly advocate you visualize your school as one large team composed of a number of smaller teams. Zenter et al. (1994), in writing about teams, notes that Walter Wriston, former CEO of Citicorp, once said, "The person that figures out how to harness the collective genius of his or her organization is going to blow the competition away" (p. 16).

Figuring out how to harness the collective genius of your school begins with identifying the key leaders and challenging them with your vision of an inclusive school and your sense of how you and they—"we"—can work together to realize that vision. Success in getting key leaders to commit to the vision will depend largely on the degree to which the principal has clearly formulated that vision and the conviction and passion with which he or she has communicated it to them. School-wide commitment to the vision, however, will be obtained only after the principal has given all stakeholders— faculty, staff, and parents—the opportunity to shape the vision, so that it becomes an expression of what they too want their school to become. Porras et al. (2007) reminds us that "for the most part, extraordinary people, teams, and organizations are simply ordinary people doing ordinary things that matter to them" (p. 5).

It is imperative in fostering a culture of inclusiveness that all staff members—administrative, teaching, support—pledge that no student go through your school without feeling that the school took a sincere interest in him or her. The principal and all staff must pledge to offer as many opportunities as possible to all students who enter your school, opportunities not only to achieve academically but also to cultivate those special interests and individual talents each brings to the school. When the student finally exits the school, what would you like the student to say about your school? One way to address this question is for the staff to complete a statement such as that

FIGURE 2.11 Student Exit Statement

When a student leaves our school, either by graduation, promotion, or moving to another area, we hope that he or she, reflecting on the experience we have offered, will be able to truthfully say about our school that

_____

_____

which appears in Figure 2.11. For comparison, a version of the statement can then be given to students when they leave, asking them for their final impressions of your school.

A similar statement could be developed and used as an exit survey given to students when they withdraw from or leave the school.

The Courage to Be an Advocate for All Students

One could argue that courage does not become evident until one confronts an obstacle, a roadblock, a challenge. School principals face obstacles every day, ranging from a discontented staff member, a reluctant teacher, a hampering provision or rule in the union contract, an irate parent, a restrictive administrative regulation, or a stifling governing-board policy or state law. There are pressures to take overt action and pressures to abstain from action.

Courage in time of war was best described by Winston Churchill (1940) when, on June 4, 1940, before the British House of Commons, he said, "We shall go on to the end, we shall fight in France, we shall fight on the seas and oceans, we shall defend our Island, whatever the cost may be . . . we shall never surrender." Courage in time of political unrest is best evidenced, one might say, by the "I Have A Dream" speech delivered by Rev. Dr. Martin Luther King on August 28, 1963, on the steps of the Lincoln Memorial, in the shadow of the great emancipator. Consider for a moment the courage it took for Dr. King to deliver that address. Also, consider the courage of President Ronald Reagan when, standing at the Brandenburg Gate in Berlin, Germany, on June 12, 1987, he challenged Mikhail Gorbachev to open the gate and tear down the wall. For whatever reason—fear, "common sense," anticipation of adverse public opinion—you may believe that you cannot address the central office, superintendent, governing board, parent group, or faculty with an issue, problem, or recommendation. If the issue affects the potential success or future of one student or a group of students and the school leader has a strategy by which to resolve the issue, advocacy demands that courageous action be taken.

Courage to some is scaling the highest peak in the Himalayas. To others, it is diving to deep coral reefs, charging up a flight of stairs into a burning World Trade Center, or engaging others in the field of combat. In our profession, courage as a student advocate in an inclusive school is the fortitude to stand up for what is right and for what is in the best interests of the student.

What obstacles to advocating for your students have you faced in your experience as a principal? Could it be a governing board policy, an administrative regulation, a community pressure group, a teacher, a clerk, a central-office staff member, the teachers' union, or even a state law? Perhaps there is a group of parents who feel strongly that the coach of their children's athletic team should be removed because he or she is "not a good coach." Courageous behavior in this instance might dictate that the principal listen to the parents but refrain from action until there is adequate evidence either that the coach should be replaced or the parents' complaints discounted.

A CASE OF COURAGE

Mr. H. has been a school principal for eighteen years. Early in his career, he was selected for a relatively new school, of which he was the third principal. Because he had been employed from outside the district, he was relatively unknown to faculty, staff, and community. He recalls that when he came to the school, morale was low and school identity fairly nonexistent. There was little accountability and no real expectations of the students, staff, or community. He determined to begin by building pride and establishing a standard of excellence in instruction and in campus life.

It took courage for a young and unknown principal to move toward the vision he had for the school. One of his first objectives was to set high expectations for teacher performance. That message began to resonate among the staff. In the first four years of his principalship, eight teachers chose to transfer, resign, or be subject to termination. Without exception, this occurred after a thorough evaluation and remediation process. Mr. H's courage was particularly evident in the case of one teacher. The veteran had been on an improvement plan a number of times during her career, but no principal had carried out the plan to its culmination. It was obvious to the parents and the teacher's peers that she struggled in many ways and was not there for her students. It was not uncommon for parents of her students to complain to Mr. H., and even the teacher's peers were not happy with her performance, particularly her relationship with her students. The staff knew that Mr. H. tried very hard to assist the teacher the first two or three years he was at the school. When it was evident that improvement was not forthcoming, Mr. H. took the appropriate steps and the teacher was released from her contract. This was not an easy undertaking for Mr. H. As he expressed, he struggled with the idea that this teacher was going to be deprived of her income. But he felt he had to take action, because the students deserved a better experience. His commitment to students, his advocacy for their well-being, was evident in this case.

Summary

This chapter has emphasized that an inclusive school addresses the needs, interests, dreams, and goals of every student that enters the school and that the principal must become the chief advocate for those students. Whether or not the school becomes inclusive depends on the principal. The principal is the key factor, the major influence, and the driving force behind the school becoming inclusive. An inclusive school demands that the needs, desires, goals, and interests of each and every student are addressed by every staff member, faculty member, and administrator. The values, beliefs, and vision for the school expressed by the principal send a clear message concerning student advocacy and inclusiveness, as do the ways he or she involves major stakeholders in the school's operation.

We have emphasized the importance of teams and team building as a key strategy toward achieving an inclusive school. A school that advocates for students will have a student advocacy process in place that will trigger quick action to address a student's problem. The process of team building begins with the principal identifying core values and beliefs as they relate to education and the school. Second, the principal must develop a vision for the school that incorporates inclusiveness. Third, the principal's values and beliefs as well as his or her vision are shared with the leadership group. Subsequent meetings with the entire faculty and staff, to share, discuss, and obtain full commitment to the core values, beliefs, and vision, are vital if the school is to become inclusive.

The vision of what the school is to become is the overriding inspiration for the principal and the faculty and staff. However, before the principal can know how to get to where he or she aspires to be, it is essential that he or she carefully analyze the school in light a number of factors. It is quite important for the school to examine current conditions related to inclusiveness. Once the analysis is completed, implementation strategies can be devised. In conjunction with those strategies, measures must be identified for determining the degree to which the school has achieved its goal of becoming inclusive.

Throughout the school year, in many kinds of circumstances, implicitly the principal and staff are continuously being asked to consider these questions: Why do we exist as a school? What do we believe in? What is our goal, and are we moving toward it? What should stakeholder involvement look like? Are our teams functioning effectively? What are we doing that is achieving the desired results? An inclusive school that provides opportunities for all students, with a principal who advocates for each and every student, is one where learning, growth, and development happens, and it is a school destined for success. In the final analysis, we share Vince Lombardi's belief that "any man's finest hours—his greatest fulfillment of all that he holds dear—is that moment when he has worked his heart out in good cause and lies exhausted on the field of battle—victorious" (Lombardi, 2010). Our field of battle may be the office, the classroom, the playground, a parent-teacher meeting, the negotiating table, or the board room. Victory will be measured by how we have improved the future of every student who has spent time with us in our school.

Application Exercises

1. Now you have made the decision to become an even stronger advocate for students. Beginning next Monday, student advocacy will become an overriding consideration in your role as principal. Generate a list of questions such as the following: What can I do to demonstrate that I am going to do everything in my power to make sure that every student succeeds at my school? How might my behavior change? How can I get the message through to all personnel in my school? Will my conversation change and, if so, how? Should there be an emphasis in faculty meetings on student advocacy? Should there be a "student advocacy" team formed to explore additional strategies to advocate for students? Are we doing all we can to make sure that no student "falls through the cracks?"

2. List the names of all your faculty and staff personnel. Using the categories given in Figure 2.9 (page 42) as a starting point, identify "school teams" at your school. Create additional teams reflecting the demographics or unique characteristics of your school. As the "coach" of your "school teams," analyze and evaluate the particular interests, talents, and skills of your faculty and staff and insert their names under the appropriate school-team heading. Share the concept with your faculty and staff and impress upon them that your objective is to create a "school-team umbrella" under which all students will find an activity in which they can participate, have fun, develop, and enjoy success. Encourage them to add additional "teams" that they think will appeal to students and give them the opportunity to opt out of or into other "school teams."

3

The Principal as an Advocate for Student Services

A PRINCIPAL'S THOUGHTS

The night turns into morning. Waking and feeling as though progress has been made in at least one area of my responsibility—evaluating teachers in an efficient and effective manner that ensures students are being taught by proven instructional strategies and by teachers who are competent in their subject areas and passionate about student-centered learning. Well, that is a mouthful. Anyhow, let me get up and get started. I have some time to get some exercise this morning before arriving at school by 7:30 a.m. As I run, I think that Ms. Dangerfield is going to be upset about my observation record of her class yesterday. The department's instructional leader and I have communicated to her the importance of incorporating instructional strategies that engage students with content. Did she not see at least two students sleeping? The poor kids were doing all that they could not to nod off. The students listened to her talk for over thirty minutes without any learning guide, collaborative work, or opportunities to mentally or physically engage with the content of her lecture. Wow! I struggled to stay awake myself. She has been given suggestions as to how to increase student involvement in her classes; yet she creates a lesson for her observation that directly contradicts what has been recommended. Well, the meeting at 9:20 a.m. will be interesting. I will share my sense of the positives in her lesson, but I must also point out areas that are weak, because the students in my school must have leadership that will not allow ineffective teachers to inhibit student learning. I am responsible and I must advocate for my students. Humph, I am almost home. Once again, I was very productive on the road.

Principals that are advocates for students must insist that all students are learning, in all classes in the school. There must be a system in place that guarantees student-centered learning every day. Students rely on adults approximately 70 percent of their lives during childhood, if not more. As the principal, you must recognize how much you impact learning. Principal pupil advocates develop a culture in their schools of continuing professional development for all staff. Professional development for teachers must include training that motivates them to use teaching strategies that have been provided by the school's leadership. Before professional development is provided, advocates make sure that teachers have provided input and that data support the need for specific kinds of training. Trust teachers to teach from their expertise, using proven instructional strategies. Provide genuine praise of good performance, often. Be sure to observe teachers during instruction; evaluate formally and informally. If you are not in and out of classes often, you are not advocating for the students in your school.

Figure 3.1 lists student services that are commonly found on school campuses. The way in which the responsibilities that lie with these individuals and offices are fulfilled is very important to the culture of your school. The titles may change, and the responsibilities may shift somewhat, but the functions are necessary to meet the needs of the school community.

First Impressions Make a Big Difference

It is extremely important that as principal you acknowledge the people who are responsible for the first impression the school community has of your campus. From the very beginning, when students and parents are registering, the student-services staff makes an impression, positive or negative. You only have one chance to make a first impression. If it is negative, it is almost impossible to recover. If it is positive, you gain ten steps to the good. Many important individuals provide the one and only first impression. Your staff must assume the same responsibility for service that you do. Exemplary behaviors must be exhibited. The student-services staff must deliver positive, correct, and competent communication. They must display the service-oriented behaviors that parents and incoming students deserve. Time must not be wasted; actions must be expedient and purposeful. Consistent and correct information must be readily available and frequently asked questions anticipated. Principal advocates place students in courses that meet their interests and needs; paperwork must not inhibit parents and students or inconvenience them to the point of frustration. The staff that works with entering students and their parents must be trained and supervised, with stress on how important their service is to the whole school community,

FIGURE 3.1 Student Services Commonly
Available on a School Campus

Administrative Services

Administrative Assistance
Intervention Specialist
Student Services Specialist
Receptionist
Health Services
Food Services
Student Welfare and Safety

Guidance and Counseling Services

Guidance Counselors
Attendance Coordinator
Behavior Interventionist
Academic Coach
Career and Technical Services Counselor
Testing Services
School Psychologist

Community Support Services

Social Services
Juvenile Probation/Child Protective Services
Psychological Testing/Counseling Services
Campus Security Personnel
Occupational Service Information

including teachers and other staff. Without reminders of their importance and value, there is the danger that they will view their jobs as routine, rather than crucial for setting and maintaining a tone supportive of student achievement. All the administrative and academic functions involved in welcoming and enrolling students must work together to provide a great start for all and an encouraging nudge toward student success and positive working relationships with families.

When students, parents, and teachers are given the tools and resources to ensure a successful start to the school year, trust in the school will increase. Constant positive feedback to staff members for good performance must be given, especially to those who are making great attempts to maintain the school culture. All staff members want to know that they are appreciated in their roles and are competent to fill in when others are absent. Remind staff how critical they are to the school community, with specific examples of actions that help to sustain the school. Motivate staff members to perform their best every day and offer them an environment that is safe and allows them to make positive contributions to the school culture. Emphasize that their best encourages the best in others.

Shared Skills (Cross Training)

Cross training alleviates challenges arising from staff absences. Having skilled staff in all positions on a daily basis ensures that students and the community are well served. Competent staff creates satisfied clients. As with certified staff, student-services staff must be secure enough to participate in professional growth opportunities. An effective school program is one that increases the knowledge and skills of both students and adults. When all people on a school campus grow and learn, students are provided models of learning that inspire achievement.

STORY OF JUANEKA

Making an Impression

Juaneka is a junior and a fourth-hour student assistant in the front office. While she waits for her next task, she has a moment to relax. Juaneka notices that Mrs. Brown seems frustrated. She realizes that Mrs. Brown is sitting at Mrs. Anderson's desk and that Mrs. Brown is visibly perturbed with the computer system, which Mrs. Anderson generally handles with ease. A parent enters and waits near Mrs. Brown's seat. The parent softly attempts to gain Mrs. Brown's attention: "Excuse me . . . " At this point, Mrs. Brown looks up with vengeance, rudely responds to the parent with an acknowledgement that says, "Can you not see that I am busy?" The parent responds with a poignant, "I need my son, and I am here to check him out." All of the negativity that the staff person exudes toward the parent, and the parent's response, rebounds onto a student, who sits awaiting direction. "Juaneka," Mrs. Brown angrily directs, "You do not have anything to do, take this pass to D141 and let her son know that his mother is waiting for him." From her desk and seated, Mrs. Brown says to the mother, "Next time call ahead and he will be here waiting for you." "I did call ahead," the mother says, "but apparently you did not receive the message." After a few moments, Juaneka realizes that Mrs. Brown had been attempting, unsuccessfully, to get the phone messages off of the phone system.

This is an example of how students are impacted by front-office staff's inability to fulfill alternate assignments and the resulting negative impression given parents and students. While this type of experience may seem to be distant from most students, such incidents can undermine a school's culture of service.

Attendance Coordinator: A Role Much Greater Than Mere Accounting

Principal student advocates create an attendance monitoring system that includes staff, is innovative, is conscience of school policies, and incorporates strategies to promote student retention. The principal must articulate a sound philosophy, one that stresses the importance of students being educated at school. Regarding attendance, principals all too often deliver a message to children and their parents that if they do not fall in the "perfect" range then they cannot attend "this school." More often than not, students then take the consequences for matters that are out of their control. Up to the age of seventeen or so, children have little direct control over their immediate circumstances. The school can make a difference, by allowing for the student's particular situation, or contribute to his or her powerlessness. Which type school do you want to lead? One that throws children away when they do not fit the "norm," or one that intervenes so that children cannot choose to lose? Understanding that there may be a few instances of failure, principal advocates align school programs with the best research relevant to increasing student retention. Parent support and communication must be integrated into program decisions, not overlooked, regardless of any perceived lack of parenting skills.

Advocate principals concern themselves with the future for each child, imagining the society into which that child will enter, with or without an education. If an attendance monitoring program is quick to remove students from school, it runs counter to a belief in the importance of educated kids. Students at risk need a purpose to attend school. It is the educational leader's responsibility to create purpose and educate each child into an independent, responsible adult. Students with attendance issues have learned that school is not necessary or important to their lives. Leaders sometimes think that at-risk students are the problem, but they are misplacing the blame. Asking the following questions will provide a clearer picture of the at-risk student's perception of school: Are the classes offered meaningful and relevant? Does every child have relationships that support areas where he or she is gifted? Are the adults developing relationships with students and providing programs that connect kids? Does everyone on campus believe that failure is not an option? Is the leadership eager and willing to reach out to families, without judgment, and provide support systems on and off campus? Are there viable safety nets/interventions that identify at-risk students before they are unreachable? If you are asking these questions and then answering positively, your student advocacy behavior is showing.

Relevant Courses Support Student Achievement

Educational research supports the notion that relevant courses motivate student achievement. This is no surprise, nor is it a novel idea. In the past, connecting student learning to purpose was often not a consideration. For most students, attending school meant just that, "attendance." Attending school was an expectation and a legal requirement. School was a safe place for kids to learn how to read, to write, and to do math. Society did not demand much more. Many acquired only a high school diploma, which was enough to provide for their families quite well. Today, for careers that provide above-average income, the demand is for workers who can do calculus, write publishable prose, and deliver presentations in three languages. Schools must provide rigorous instruction relevant to these changing demands. Gone are the days when students wanted to learn for learning sake, as was often the case especially for adult students. The principal must be the instructional leader who provides courses that develop the skills necessary for the twenty-first century; he or she must monitor what is taught and take responsibility for students' lack of interest in attending school.

Relationships That Support Giftedness

Each student is gifted in some way. The principal must identify areas of giftedness and create strategies for students to connect and grow. No matter how small or large a school is, people need to connect with others. This is human nature. All children do not fit the same mold. Faculty, staff, students, and administrators must listen to children individually to assess their needs, observe the cultures that exist, and be mindful of the different people that need to be served every day at school. Positive and supportive relationships for all children do not happen accidently. Often, what students need is overheard or observed during the school day. The principal advocate listens astutely to students; he or she observes them to learn how to serve them.

When you use your ears to hear and eyes to see critically, you will be more able to discern what relationships are thriving and which are not surviving.

Principal student advocates through their actions have the ability to make each child on campus believe that he or she is important. They make eye contact with each student that passes and attend a variety of activities in which their students participate. They recognize students for their accomplishments, regularly. Principal advocates acknowledge individual accomplishments as they go in and out of classrooms. They find behaviors that fit their personalities and use them to lift up students throughout the school day; these behaviors strengthen relationships on campus. Additionally, students share their experiences with the principal with other students. Principals need to intentionally reach out to all children, not only those that "fit the mold" but also those who are perceived by others as different. Principals cannot be everywhere, but they can ensure that their presence is felt by the faculty and staff. The teachers and staff must reflect the principal's leadership style, a style that creates positive relationships with students. All employees must be passionate for children and want to work with students not only in the classroom but also outside.

Failure Is Not an Option

In schools, there are some things that are optional. Failure cannot be an option. Prior to the call for increased accountability in schools, educators did not wholly endorse this idea. Schools were places where those that chose to learn could learn. If students did not want to learn in school settings, as young adults they commonly dropped out of school and entered the work force.

Today, with advances in technology that necessitate high-order thinking skills in the workplace, a high-school diploma is often not enough to acquire a good job, one with a secure future. Failing in school is thus definitely not an option. Therefore principals have a responsibility to make certain that all students are motivated to complete high school and continue their professional advancement through life-long learning. Principals must create programs that guarantee success in both general areas and the specialized skills needed in particular communities. If the adults employed on your school campus are not willing to take responsibility for student-centered learning and are more prone to blame children and circumstances for education failures, you will need to educate them on the importance of education and education's effect on communities. If the adults do not buy into the philosophy that failure is not an option, encouraging them to seek a different career will do your students a great service.

When students fail, the school fails. When the school fails, it fails the children and the community in which it is embedded. When the community fails, its economy fails. When the economy fails, blame falls on the education system and ultimately our children become the scapegoats. Educating children is our obligation. Every child on a school campus must be prepared beyond basic reading, writing, and arithmetic. The educators on a school campus must take responsibility for student learning and ensure that it occurs in both the best and the worst circumstances. What the wisest and best parents in the community want for their children, the school principal and staff must provide for all.

Family Focus for Advocating for Students

In communities where families are generally comfortable with advocating for their children, there may yet be certain families who are reluctant. Regardless of individual circumstance, however, the need for a caring and understanding leader is constant. Given the opportunity to work with parents who challenge the practices and programs of the school, principals have two choices. The principal can either be offended and defensive or he or she can listen and learn. A lot of what can be learned about a child can come directly from his parents. Regardless of whether a meeting is scheduled by the principal or a drop-in visit from demanding parents, listen and learn. Have faith that the encounter will move you toward what is in the best interests of the student, toward a positive outcome. "Positive" does not mean an outcome that will necessarily make everyone happy but rather one that is best for the child. In a crisis, remain student focused. The parent will see that your actions are truly intended to benefit the child.

On occasion, a principal will have a perception that parents are apathetic because their actions appear not to support the needs of the student. The parents may choose not to call or visit the school when asked. Judging the love of parents is a waste of time and unacceptable. All parents love their children; however, some parents err in their love. Parents want the very best for their children; some are challenged to know what the best is. Some parents may not understand the value of monitoring their children's academic growth daily, but that does not mean that they do not care about their children. Principals must use a variety of communications to connect parents to their schools. Principals in impoverished communities must also maintain a focus on the family. Whether or not parents are educated, the advocate principal fosters positive relationships with families and directs all communications toward the goal of children's success in school.

STORY OF MRS. SAMPSON

Advocacy Requires Both Time and Effort

Mrs. Sampson was extremely excited about her opportunity to be the new principal at Canyon State High School (CSHS). Canyon State was located not too far from the school where she was an assistant principal. Because she had been an assistant principal for several years in the same district, she felt she had some knowledge of the school. She learned rather quickly, however, that what a school may look like from the outside may not be close to the reality within. The students at Canyon State were very wary of her. They were not as welcoming toward her as they were toward teachers that had been teaching in CSHS for a while. So, Mrs. Sampson maintained a professional attitude. She knew that she would have to learn about the students on this new and unfamiliar campus. Very seldom were there parents in the front office meeting with teachers. If parents were on campus, it was because they were picking up students or signing them in to school. Visits did occur when students misbehaved and were required to leave the campus under the authority of parents or legal guardians.

In the month of January, before registration, parents of new students were asked to attend an open house. Parents of only fifty of the potential three hundred students enrolling arrived. Extensive planning and preparation by maintenance staff, teachers, sponsors, coaches, and administration had been undertaken—all for an event that ultimately served fifty parents. Afterward, Mrs. Sampson thought extensively about the purpose of the meeting. In the end, it provided an invaluable opportunity to reflect on the importance of educating parents and students about their school—the place where students will spend most of their days over several years. She realized that the event, as planned, continued mostly for political reasons. All schools in the district provided this service; the expectations were the same for all schools. After meeting with the school leadership, it was decided that the parent community did not benefit from this mode of delivery.

Mrs. Sampson implemented multiple means of communication to help parents fully understand the value of selecting a school that houses programs to enhance their children's opportunities. She created relationships with the feeder schools and attended parent meetings off campus. Mrs. Sampson went periodically to a middle-school campus and gave motivational presentations to incoming youth. At school-community events, Mrs. Sampson went out of her way, after the school day and on the weekends, to become acquainted, in hopes of creating relationships that would encourage parents to take ownership of their school, make suggestions toward improvement, and provide input concerning course offerings. As time went on, when parents arrived on campus to check their children in and out of school, they also made an effort to say hello to Mrs. Sampson. The children began to relate to Mrs. Sampson. No longer was she a foreigner. Students invited her to family and community events. She began to become a part of the community, and the community embraced her as one of their own.

People motivate each other. Principals have the power to move school communities toward what is best for each and every child, but first the community must know that you are family-focused.

Interventions Fostering Student Success

Principal student advocates assess the needs of the school community. School data are analyzed to determine if existing programs are meeting the goals of the school. School data must determine what programs and instruction are needed to ensure academic success for all children. Too often, leaders are criticized because of the perception that they believe that any new program will work in all schools. Unfortunately, principals have sometimes been guilty of incorporating programs simply because they represent the "latest thing" in education. Principals must be well informed about the many possible interventions that produce positive results; however, they must be very careful not to move too quickly, without adequate support from instructional leaders on campus. Keeping up with case studies of successful reform in schools and participating in professional development workshops are ways to hone your judgment as to the tools that may be most useful on a school campus. Be mindful; not all programs work everywhere.

School goals are derived from data, vision, and wisdom. Data must determine the possible interventions. Visionary is what the student advocate must be. Wisdom is to know how to actualize. Programs must have measures of efficacy. If the data do not show positive results after two full years of implementation, the principal may need to alter or terminate the program. Schools do not have time to hope for success if progress is not evident. Principals must take risks and allow the staff to take risks, but not at the expense of educational regress.

Interventions must not be punitive. They must be presented as opportunities for students to grow. As students are invited to participate in new programs, they will recognize that improvement is desired in certain areas and understand the intended benefits of the change. A clearly descriptive initial presentation is the key to a successful implementation. The presentation should show that there must be graduated levels of achievement. The students in the program must feel as though accomplishments are acknowledged. Whether you are implementing behavior modification programs in the area of attendance, social behavior, or academic achievement, stages of accomplishment and celebration will encourage those involved and motivate others to get involved.

In response to behavioral problems, negative consequences for the student may unfortunately sometimes be necessary. If this is the only option, however, a sustained change in behavior is not to be expected. Negative consequences have not proven to change behavior in the long term. Children find themselves in difficult situations and make poor decisions for all types of reasons. Providing alternative choices and pointing to assistance programs will be very helpful to some students, while others remain uninterested. Those that would like another chance to change their circumstances deserve that chance. Do not place students in programs that do not promise appropriate benefits. Instead, place students in the best possible position to be successful. The supervising adult in intervention programs must be one that students respect, one who is trustworthy, and one who understands the importance of treating students fairly, while the same time maintaining high expectations of all participants. Additionally, this adult must maintain communication with parents of the students involved.

Unintentional outcomes can come with school-day intervention programs. The intervention becomes more attractive to challenged students. Rather than attempting to make the adjustments necessary for success in a "normal" setting, students turn to the alternative. Realize that not all students are successful in normal school settings, but what is important is what is learned when students are given the tools to be successful. When rigorous and relevant content is taught, when every student experiences sound and meaningful relationships, when failure is not an option, when leadership focuses on the importance of families, and when support networks are in place, more students will be served individually than not. When you as principal, as the advocate for all children, have these prerequisites in place, the educational and life goals you hold for your own children will come into reach be for other people's children as well.

STORY OF MR. KARSTEN

The Results of Advocacy Are Not Always Immediate

Mr. Karsten was visiting a community center, located in the inner city, where his son was trying out for a club basketball team. The community center hosts many after-school and evening activities for youth and young adults. As he observes the tryout, a young African-American man approaches him. Mr. Karsten recognizes him and stands to greet him. The young man was a student on a campus where Mr. Karsten was principal. Memories come flooding back. Mr. Karsten recalls this young man's face as a student; he never smiled and seemed to be very unhappy and always troubled. Belonging to a gang only made things worse for him. He was often suspended for fighting or being asked to stay home until things cooled down on a campus that posed a threat to him and others because of people with whom he was associated. As a student his physique was unbelievable; he could have been an outstanding high-school athlete. However, the choices he made while in school interfered with his achievement and he eventually dropped out.

Returning to the present, Mr. Karsten looks into the eyes of a smiling young man who is physically fit and very interested in talking. He begins to tell Mr. Karsten that he appreciated all that he tried to do for him while in school. He says that he has been waiting for an opportunity to see him again, to thank him. The young man shares that he has taken up professional boxing, has completed a GED, and is currently attending school; he seems very happy about his choices. He is extremely excited to share that he is getting married in the near future. After his former student acknowledges how proud he is of his accomplishments, Mr. Karsten leaves very pleased and with a full heart—pleased indeed that this young man never gave up, that he found purpose in his life, and chose alternate paths. He relishes the thought that he has contributed to the success a former student has found.

Guidance Services: Advocating for Student Success

Students perform at various levels. Students with great academic skills need motivating just as student with low skills do. Some students have great skills, but perform at low levels. Some students have low skills and perform even lower than they might. Certain ethnic groups are assumed by some to be more academically talented than others, and the genders are often considered differently, in terms of the expectations for performance. All students need an opportunity for success. It is ultimately the responsibility of the principal to provide supportive systems for all students. A place on school campuses that assists in this responsibility is the guidance office. Counselors try to understand what motivates each student, as well as his or her skills and desires. "When you're doing things right," writes one, "it's like you're another parent, except they trust you a little more. Individuals who aspire to enter the field should be aware that emotional as well as intellectual demands come with the territory. As most guidance counselors spend over a third of their time in consultations with students and parents, prospective counselors should be comfortable with teenagers and have excellent communication skills" (Princeton Review, 2010, p. 1).

Some highly trained educators, including some who had been teachers, obtained their masters in guidance counseling degrees to serve students in a different capacity. The school principal must be careful to create a guidance department full of individuals who are there for children, and not to work less. There are teachers who become interested in counseling because of a belief that less is required as compared to teaching. It is your responsibility as principal to protect students from educators who have no desire to work hard to achieve what is best for children. The guidance department must be visionary and anticipate the kinds of support needed by youth today. Counselors are not highly paid clerical workers, but rather professionals trained to learn strengths of students and to place them in settings appropriate to their individual educational goals. The counselor must understand the values of the school community and community at large. None in the staff can have the mindset that only "this type" of student can enter "these classes "and "those students" must enroll in "these types" of classes. Allowing teachers to limit a student's opportunities is not acceptable. As principal, you must empower teachers and counselors to make sure that students are able to walk through as many doors as possible after graduating from high school. What you expect for your own children's education is what must be provided for the children on your campus. Every student must be given multiple opportunities to establish paths towards postsecondary education. While many may not clearly know their direction, they must have many options.

STORY OF MISS HOWARD

Stepping into the Shoes of Students in Need

Sammy had been a Division 1 basketball prospect before entering high school. He is 6′5″ and very athletic. His freshman year was a struggle. As he transitioned into high school there were major gaps in his study skills and academic work ethic. Teachers from the middle school spoke poorly about his academic performance and were outspoken about how Sammy and his parents were deluded about his prospects in basketball, because of his lack of attention to academics. After learning these things, the school's counselors accepted the low expectations and did not act to put the young man on a path of success.

His first year, he ended up with a 1.8 grade point average. His performance was consistent with his history in middle school; no more was expected. No one in the guidance office intervened. Before Sammy's sophomore year, the principal hired a new guidance counselor, Miss Howard. Miss Howard was a scholarship athlete during her undergraduate years. She was an exceptional softball player for University of Southern California. She remembers how important her high-school counselor was to her. Because of her high-school counselor's attention to scholarship opportunities for her and to her future career, she was inspired to become a teacher and, now, a high-school guidance counselor. The principal hired her specifically to assist students in excelling in areas in which they were gifted, to encourage placement of all students in rigorous classes, and to create opportunities for students to be awarded academic and athletic scholarships.

At the beginning of the school year, Miss Howard met Sammie in a history class. She heard him talking with students around him; he was sharing with students that he played in a major basketball tournament over the weekend and was named MVP of the tournament.

Well, she thought, "That is impressive." Before class ended, she asked Sammie if he would come to the guidance office during lunch, to discuss colleges he might attend. Sammie did just that. Miss Howard shared a bit of her background with him. He in turn was impressed with her background. Miss Howard asked Sammie what his goals and plans for the future were. The athlete said that he would like to play basketball in college one day. With that, Miss Howard retrieved his academic records and informed Sammie that he would need to improve his grade-point average and perform well on either the ACT or SAT. They continued discussing his career goals and other topics of interest. Before long, Sammie was informed about scholarship opportunities, meetings were scheduled to create an academic plan for his coming years, study-skills training sessions begun, and communications initiated with colleges of interest. Sammie had been placed in great hands—those of someone who cared enough to do more than the minimum. Miss Howard did what was natural and appropriate; she met a student where he was, gave him confidence and the tools to be successful, in spite of others who had done nothing but set him up for guaranteed failure. Why did Miss Howard do this? She had a background similar to Sammie's. She had sought out a career helping students toward excellence in school and postsecondary education. Certainly, she could have waited in her office for students to ask for assistance. The minimum is enough for some, but it is not acceptable on a school campus. As principal, identifying the needs of students and hiring qualified staff in the guidance office to counsel students toward goals beyond school are requisite steps toward creating a system that supports students every day of the year.

Rigor for All

Principals today face many challenges. Given the accountability called for in schools today, leaders often experience consequences because they lose focus. A major challenge facing most American schools is closing the achievement gap. Every principal must challenge the school community to research student performance, identify trends, and develop action plans to increase achievement in all children, especially within populations that are not performing well. Students who are academically challenged are often placed in least restrictive environments, without those supports provided by state departments. At the other end of the spectrum are gifted students, for whom there are also mandates, such as individual learning plans for students who exceed specified scores on standardized tests. However, students that do not fall within the bounds of Individuals with Disabilities Education Act (IDEA) or gifted status are often left in limbo. Historically, minority children have performed the lowest on most school campuses. We can speculate as to the reasons why, but strategically a principal advocate can make a difference and close the gap by embedding rigorous coursework for all children.

"Rigor refers to academic rigor—learning in which students demonstrate a thorough, in-depth mastery of challenging tasks to develop cognitive skills through reflective thought, analysis, problem-solving, evaluation, or creativity" (International Center for Leadership in Education, 2010, p. 4).

The guidance department can incorporate strategies to give students an opportunity to enroll in honors, gifted, and advanced-placement courses simply by asking them to do so. When leadership accepts the norm, the norm is exactly what is achieved, resulting in average performance. The principal is required to advocate for all children. Counselors can be the most immediate advocates. In some cases, very talented minority students with excellent records enroll in regular classes. Often, these students did not think of enrolling in more rigorous courses, for lack of adult encouragement. An identification method should also be in place for students who have the required skills and knowledge but have performed poorly on an entrance exam and have enrolled in courses that are not challenging. If a child does not attain the required entrance score on stratification tests, alternate means of affording entrance need to be established, to ensure the children with poor test-taking skills the chance to be challenged, not penalized, when the ability or skill level is there. Principals cannot fear to do what is best for children.

STORY OF MR. BROWN

Creating Opportunities for All Students

Mr. Brown is the head of the guidance department of a local middle school. Year after year, he has placed African-American boys with low reading scores into special reading classes. He recognized that many of the boys were capable because their class grades were above average. He asked himself, "What is the deal?" Mr. Brown decided to visit the reading class one day. When he entered he saw what should not have been surprising, a class full of brown and academically talented faces.

Having the data to support an alternate placement for these boys, he scheduled an appointment with the principal and asked the principal to take a walk with him to the reading lab. Mr. Brown shared his thoughts with his principal and asked if he could invite the students who have performed well in the other classes to enroll in honors courses. Mr. Brown and the principal were in agreement that teachers would create a welcoming environment for new honors students and students with teacher recommendations and that their presence in classes would not inhibit rigorous instruction for all. They believed that this tactic would help close the achievement gap, that these teachers would challenge this group of students to excel in the new setting. The principal was ecstatic! Embracing the idea and strategizing how to create opportunities for other children, he found that soon more and more minority children were enrolling in honors courses in middle schools and on into the high schools. The principal's willingness to listen to his staff, to allow for creativity and to implement a program that met individual needs amounted to a very effective leadership strategy. Some of these students never would have thought to take courses at the honors level. Why? Because no one ever asked.

Counselor roles in schools must be seen as critical. The counselor's office cannot be the place where teachers want to work when they no longer want to teach. The principal is responsible for hiring counselors who are passionate about implementing innovative programs that give students what is necessary to be successful in and outside of school. The people in these positions must truly embrace the importance of their role. Question 6, in the Student Advocacy Traits assessment in Chapter 1, addresses what a principal should do with a student who needs guidance and a positive option. Refer to Question 6, which one did you choose? The example with Miss Howard and the success of Terrance is a great example of why principals must hire educators to be student advocates. The principal cannot be directly connected to all children, but he or she has the responsibility to hire advocates who can and will directly advocate for them.

Expect the Unexpected

Over a weekend, there was a huge party at a student's home. Over two hundred people attended. Most were underage drinkers who soon became intoxicated. Susan was at the party. Before long, she was completely intoxicated; she walked into a pool that was full of people, slipped and hit her head on the side of the pool, and lay unconscious at the bottom of the pool. Finally, a boy realizes that someone is face down in the pool. The kids quickly called emergency services, but it was too late; Susan had drowned. Given a horrible event such as this, what steps should a principal take to ensure that students have support at school on Monday? Who will need to learn the facts of what happened? Who will speak with the parents of students in attendance at the party? Will there be discipline involved? What is the appropriate manner in which the principal should behave?

Principal advocates create crisis communication plans for catastrophic events on or off campus. Plans must be aligned with district policies and procedures, to ensure that regardless of the issue, students and staff are provided counsel by supportive personnel. When situations on campus become stressful and emotionally taxing to teachers, students, and staff, it is the principal's responsibility to ensure that their needs are met emotionally, mentally, and socially. Distressing unexpected events create disquiet in minds of children.

The principal must anticipate the challenges that would come with such events and plan for the safety of all on campus.

Other services are often found in the guidance office. Depending on the district, community programs may be housed on the school site. Educational services are often led by a teacher on special assignment or a certified staff person charged with providing services for certain groups, such as "English limited learners," gifted students, and students with disabilities. Regardless of the program, however, the principal must clearly communicate the need to create an environment where parents, students, teachers, counselors, and staff together serve students and guide them toward fulfilling individual learning plans.

Community Social Services

Often students need support from or are involved with other agents of the community. Whether these are child protective services (CPS) workers, juvenile probation officers, or police investigators, schools must be willing to assist and to provide access to students during the school day. Professional inquiries as to why these organizations need access to students will place you in a better position to serve students when they are questioned. Because of your knowledge of students' behavior on campus, you may already have some idea of the matter. Regardless of the issue, the principal must not judge students, but rather advocate for them.

STORY OF MRS. HAMPTON

Things Do Not Always Go Smoothly

While Mrs. Hampton, the principal of Washington High School, replies to emails in her office, Mark, a student, walks in. She turns around upon hearing her name. "Mrs. Hampton, this lady from CPS is here. She is being rude to me and I do not want to talk to her anymore. She told me that she is going to have me taken away because I told her I do not know what my IEP says. She cannot talk to me that way. I am trying to do my best now. I have messed up, and I am going to do better, but I do not need her to be disrespectful." Mrs. Hampton listens. Not sure what had happened, she walks into the office where Mark had been meeting with the CPS staff. After introducing herself and pleasantly greeting the visitor as a guest of Washington High School, Mrs. Hampton inquires about the meeting. The CPS staff person explains why she is at the school to speak with Mark. Additionally, she shares with Mrs. Hampton what had upset Mark. Mark was not compliant in his answers, so she asked him about his disability. Because of his flippant responses, she let him know that she is there to inform him of the penalties that may be imposed if he continues to run away from home. Before her arrival, Mark's mother had informed her that he was receiving special services but had not given her specifics as to his disability.

Mrs. Hampton does not want to interfere with the CPS staff person's duties. She informs her of previous interactions with Mark and how best to communicate with him so that he does not escalate his behavior. As she begins to leave, Mrs. Hampton informs the CPS agent that she will retrieve a copy of Mark's IEP and that it will be delivered before she leaves the school. Lastly, the principal shares with her that she will speak with Mark and explain to him the importance of complying and answering questions because, as he needs to understand, he could be taken from his home, which would jeopardize the goals that he now has for his life. The CPS staff looks at the principal intently and responds, "You know, I like you. Wow, it is a great thing that he knows that even though he misbehaves he can talk to you. You are a good principal." Mrs. Hampton thanks her and leaves the office to retrieve Mark, who is seated in her office.

Special Education and Students with Disabilities

STORY OF TERRANCE

Advocacy Accentuates the Positive

As a middle-school student, Terrance had received support from Special Services, which continued through high school. Terrance was extremely dissatisfied with the support from the special-education department, not because the services were not helpful, but because he felt they were not discreet—he did not want others to know that he was in special education and that the courses were remedial. He prefers a classroom environment that is least restrictive and requests to be placed in regular courses with support, as needed. While the special-education department chair and his assigned case worker are reluctant, considering the support of his parents, they create a regular schedule for his sophomore year, with his case manager as a contact. Terrance works extremely hard and has strong support from his parents. In October of his sophomore year, Terrance takes the state assessment and passes all three required areas: reading, mathematics, and writing. Everyone is really proud of him. As his sophomore year continues, Terrance begins to advocate for himself in his individual education plan meetings and in his classes. His doctor diagnosed him as having an attention deficit disorder. Terrance recognizes weakness in terms of focusing and processing information. He also has difficulty with retention of material. The professional staff recommends additional testing to gain full assessment of his challenges. After a battery of tests and varied instructional strategies, it is determined that Terrance performs best when given more time to read material, when notes are provided in classes, and when tests are "chunked." Although Terrance's reading scores on assignments are below grade level, his class grades at the end of the year are well above average, and it is recommended that he transition into 504 status. As a 504 student, Terrance continues to excel academically. His confidence increases along with his self-esteem. The 504 counselor continues to support his individual education plan. In classes, he is allowed to go straight to the guidance office to take tests. His reading teacher agrees to read all tests to him, and his math teacher emails notes from class to his home to aid with homework. This support continues through his remaining high-school years. As a 504 student, Terrance is now successfully completing his education at a university with the same accommodations.

Research shows that learning-disabled students who are classified as special-needs students do not perform significantly below their grade level in their elementary years. However, as the years continue, an achievement gap appears. This is disconcerting to educators who work for improvements, not declines, in student performance. There are multiple reasons for the widening achievement gap in performance. One is consistent experiences of failure. In the elementary years, students do not readily see deficits in learning. As time goes on, however, they become more able to identify weaknesses—their own as well as others'. Failing more often than achieving success, students with deficits begin to mask their disabilities with personally rewarding but socially disruptive behaviors. Before students learn that "success" in misbehavior is better than no success at all, the principal must make sure that the teachers closest to special-needs students are of the belief that students must be placed in least restrictive environments. Students are often placed in restrictive environments because they are then easier to assist. Students are pulled out of regular classes on multiple occasions for remedial instruction. Upon return, they commonly become outcasts and are looked upon as different. Other students start to believe that something must be wrong with these students.

In the middle-school years, teachers can more readily tell who learns quickly and who struggles. So educators tend to solidify perceptions of inadequacy, pulling some students out of the normal setting for remedial work, apart from their peers. Principal advocates understand that there are programs that benefit special-needs students and increase their performance, but they do not endorse differences in content relative to the "regular" classroom.

Continuing to do the same thing, "pulling out," beyond the middle-school years only puts students behind. Much research supports the benefits of heterogeneous grouping. Chapter 2 discusses the concept of inclusiveness in detail. Heterogeneous groups perform significantly better than homogeneous groups. Do effective heterogeneous classrooms involve much creativity and individual support? Absolutely, they do; however, if they enhance kids' self-worth, maintain high expectations, and do not kill a kids' spirit, then the heterogeneous groups are worth the effort. Principals must be knowledge-able about current research and the most programs in closing the gap for special-needs students. Students with severe disabilities need to be exposed to what are considered "regular" and advanced populations, appropriately, as well. Students with reading deficiencies need assistance in content areas, not in a reading class, in their secondary years. The more a student has the opportunity to read critically and experience success in that endeavor, the more he or she will want to read, period. Motivation to read for leisure may lag because of past experience, while what is needed is to learn the rewards of reading critically. Advocates place specialists in the regular classroom when support is needed; they do not pull students out of academic settings for the sake of convenience. Educating and leading a community of teachers and students can be quite overwhelming at times, but also very rewarding. Life is challenging all by itself; when it includes supervised practice and student choice the complications are manifold and the results not always foreseeable. The principal must be a positive influence in the lives of the children he or she serves. Leadership must not be distant from the core work of education; it must be clear, visible, and palpable to students. Especially given the high expectations now placed on educational institutions, it must be remembered that all you do is for students. Principals are in school to serve all students; students are not in school to serve adults. Given the positive examples from the headmaster on campus, effective models of developing positive relation-ships with students must be clearly present.

Summary

A myriad of examples could be given of the principal as student advocate. The principal has many responsibilities each and every day, whether on campus or in the community. In advocating for students, the goal of ensuring that all support programs and departments meet students' needs and align with the school's philosophy cannot be compromised. Student services must function exceptionally because they directly affect students every day. The principal must maintain focus on students by modeling positive and relent-less actions that gives every child a chance to be successful. Principal student advocates must believe that all students can achieve and strive every day to make success a reality for all students on campus. Figure 3.2 offers additional thoughts for the principal student advocate.

FIGURE 3.2 Thoughts for the Principal as Student Advocate

Trust those you empower to carry out the duty to meet the needs of students, parents, and the school community. This must be a priority.

Nothing can be accidental; all must be intentionally delivered to ensure success. Advocate for all children, including those who cannot advocate for themselves.

Advocate for someone else's child as you would for your own.

Take the role for which you have been well trained and add some common sense when you are contemplating, alone.

Nothing meaningful remains the same; all is worthy of positive change.

While results may seem slow to appear, when you least expect it they will visibly burst forth.

While results may seem slow to appear, when you least expect it they will visibly burst forth.

Principals must insist that teachers obtain evidence that their students have mastered new skills and knowledge. This will guarantee that contributions are made to students' personal growth.

Application Exercises

1. When a parent walks into your office after conferring with a guidance counselor or other faculty or staff, ask him or her to share with you how they were treated. Ask for genuine feedback. Share the parent's responses with staff. Share the positive and the not so positive feedback. Quality services in schools provide parents with peace of mind regarding those who are supporting their children each day.

2. Interview a college-bound student and ask her or him this question: If you were I, what additional supports would you make available to students through the guidance office? Principals that truly advocate for students need

to elicit feedback about services offered. Does the feedback give evidence that the staff is meeting your expectations?

3. Attend an upcoming class reunion and visit with alumni. As you do so, listen for evidence of support your school provided in the past to determine how the school's practices assisted students toward success in their postsecondary years.

4. If your school offers remedial classes, visit one. Determine what the diversity looks like, compare results to the demographics of your school, and ask if the population of students in remedial classes is representative of your school demographics. If you find an imbalance relative to what might be expected, develop strategies to correct it.

5. Informally walk through your honors-level courses. Evaluate the population enrolled. Check with the guidance department to learn how students are placed in classes and devise a strategy to include more students that may not have had the opportunity to be in a more rigorous class.

4

Creating an Environment for Teaching and Learning: The Student Advocate's Primary Challenge

Creating an Environment for Teaching and Learning

The principal who is a student advocate makes a personal commitment to create and maintain a school culture that maximizes the opportunities for teachers to teach and students to learn. A commitment such as this entails a number of concepts that are examined in this chapter. A well-organized school is a prerequisite. Chaos, uncertainty, or the absence of clearly defined systems and procedures undermines your cultivation of an optimal atmosphere for learning. The characteristics of an orderly campus are discussed below, along with strategies to achieve orderliness. Personal safety is always a concern of parents, students, and staff, and principals' approaches to achieving a safe campus are presented. Preventing inappropriate or disruptive student behavior in the classroom and on the campus is always a goal of the student advocate, and so initiatives to deal with such behavior are also presented, the objective always being to best serve the interests of the student involved as well as the student body as a whole.

Organized Chaos: The First Day of School

You are the principal of an elementary school; it is the first day of school, and you are standing on the sidewalk watching the fourth and fifth graders riding their new bikes to school. Parents motor through the circle drive and blow a kiss as their son or daughter gets out of the car. You greet the students with a friendly "Hello." Backpacks are new, clothes are new, there is a bounce in their step, they are smiling and looking for their friends. Some are carrying musical instruments in cases that are as big or bigger than the kids themselves. Mom or dad drives off to work. Every parent expects you and your teachers to do everything in your power to help their son or daughter have a good year in school. Now you decide to welcome the kindergartners, so you stroll down the sidewalk into the parking lot where parents have parked their cars. There they are—parents walking their little ones to their teachers. Some mothers, and perhaps some fathers, are dabbing their eyes, because for the first time they are releasing the care and nurturing of their precious child to someone else. That someone else may very well be a total stranger, someone they have never seen or met before. What do you think is going through the mind of the parent? What is the child thinking? What is that parent's hope for the child? What does the parent expect of the school?

Or perhaps you are the principal of a high school. You, too, are out on campus watching the students enter. There is not a parent in sight. Some of the kids are texting their friends, some are talking on their cell phones, some are listening to music and bobbing or weaving back and forth, keeping time. You hear the loud rumble of someone's new mufflers as he revs up the engine to announce his arrival on campus for this new year. Girls are giggling and boys are strutting and staring. As principal, this, in all likelihood, is one of the most important or stressful days of the year—the first day of school. (The second most important or stressful day, perhaps, is promotion or graduation day.) The principal has to be sure that all those students get to the right classroom and get signed in to their assigned classes, with the correct teacher. Then there is all that paperwork turned in at the end of that first day, collected by every student's last teacher, with all the appropriate signatures.

Principals believe they do everything possible to plan and execute appropriate procedures to achieve a successful and orderly first day. One principal reported that on the first day of school each year he goes to every classroom and welcomes the students back to school. He tells the students how happy he is to have them back and that he missed them while school was out. During these visits he is introduced to students new to the school. He tells them about the opportunities available to them and that he expects them to become active participants. This principal personally meets every student new to his school. He makes a personal connection, if not on the day the student enters, then within the first week of that student's enrollment. He personally is committed to the success of each student in his school. Teachers are very much aware of how important each student is to the principal. His interest and concern set the example for all teachers to follow. Teachers confirm the principal's commitment to each student and exhibit the same concern.

No matter whether the child is a kindergartner, an elementary, middle-school, or high-school student, all parents have expectations for their child they trust will be met while he or she is in your school. These include the expectation that the principal and his or her staff will view that student as important, as valuable, and with an appreciation of his or her potential, and that under your care and influence he or she will be provided with every opportunity to achieve, succeed, and grow. Parents expect the principal and his or her teachers to keep them informed of their child's progress in each class, as well as of any inappropriate behavior, either in the classroom or on campus. Informed parents is one characteristic of a totally effective school.

School Effectiveness: Creating a Desired Environment for Learning

Research abounds on the topic of school effectiveness and the characteristics of an effective school. Such characteristics, or descriptors, are often referred to as "correlates," and they include the following: clear and focused mission, frequent monitoring of student progress, safe and orderly environment, high expectations for student success, strong instructional leadership, opportunity to learn/time on task, and positive home-school relations. Although we could build a strong case for each of the correlates, our focus here is the principal's role in creating a safe and orderly environment. As Lezotte and McKee-Snyder (2011) write in *What Effective Schools Do*, "In the effective school, an orderly, purposeful, and businesslike atmosphere free from the threat of physical and emotional harm exists. The school culture and climate are conducive to teaching and learning" (p. 201). A safe and orderly environment sets the stage for and creates a conducive atmosphere for all other activities in the school.

A Safe School Environment: A High Priority for the Principal

For every parent, the most important person in your school is his or her child. The parents assume that their expectations, as described above, will be fulfilled in an environment that is safe. Parents expect you to deal promptly with a student who fails to follow the rules and who might be a threat to their child. The parents expect you to perform your duties in an effective and efficient manner. The challenge facing the principal is how to create a school that is safe for all persons at all times, orderly and free from chaos, while at the same time being a strong advocate for each student. We look to the literature on effective schools and examine the strategies of principals of such schools.

One perspective on a safe and orderly school environment is that it is characterized by the *absence* of negative or undesirable student behaviors, such as fighting, bullying, vandalism, threats, and graffiti. From another perspective, a safe and orderly environment is characterized by the *presence* of positive or desirable behaviors, on the part of both students and faculty. It is the principal who leads the charge for the second kind, as he or she emphasizes the types of behaviors expected of all faculty, staff, and students.

So, how does the principal who is a student advocate build a safe and secure learning environment and prevent behaviors detrimental to school safety? One principal interviewed believes that the goal of school safety can be achieved, in part, by getting parents and the community involved. He wants his school to be the centerpiece of community pride. He creates opportunities for parents to get "plugged in" and involved in their son's or daughter's education. Parental involvement is "nonnegotiable," he claims. He knows that involving parents in as many school events or activities as possible will help garner the support he needs to create and maintain a safe school environment. He also knows that the very presence of parents at his school, the visibility of volunteers on campus, has a calming effect on students and minimizes undesirable behaviors.

Opportunities for parental participation at his school include the "Family Fall Festival," "Fall Curriculum Night," "Family Spring BBQ," "Art Masterpiece Gallery," and the Running Club. The Running Club, for example, is an after-school event for students in all grades that occurs several times during the year. A course is carefully laid out through the community's neighborhoods. Teachers, parents, and even grandparents participate by running along with students. Other adults (parents, grandparents, community residents) volunteer by stationing themselves at strategic points along the course, for safety, to provide water or an energy snack, and to direct the runners. The event is a quite visible extension of the school into the community and, as a positive experience shared by students and community members, it builds goodwill, appreciation, and respect between the school and the community.

Principals expect faculty and staff to recognize, support, and reward good behavior. Awards and other types of recognition contribute to job satisfaction, commitment, and morale. Employee-of-the-month programs for certified and noncertified staff are an effective technique for building pride, confidence, collegiality, and cooperation. The recognition need not be expensive or elaborate. The story is told of Tom Watson, CEO of IBM, who, when given an idea by one of his employees that impressed him greatly, felt he should reward the employee in some way. He gave the employee the only thing he had in his desk at that moment—a banana. That moment led to IBM instituting its Top Banana award—a lapel pin worn with pride by the employee who contributed a timely and significant idea. During Watson's tenure, the Top Banana award became very prestigious and coveted. Principals who are not already doing so should consider something similar, such as a "Big Apple," "Golden Apple," or "Special Apple" award, permanent or traveling, given to the employee exhibiting some special behavior during a predetermined period of the school year.

One exemplary student advocate principal goes so far as to make physical modifications, as he puts it, to his campus to recognize the accomplishments of students and staff. Banners are hung recognizing academic excellence. An art-masterpiece gallery displays examples of student artwork. Bulletin boards and display cases with pictures of students and their work abound around the campus.

A Safe School Environment: Creating a Family Atmosphere

In creating an environment ideally conducive to learning, one must consider not only the safety of students but also the extent to which the school's procedures are organized, understood, and followed. There are two components to a safe and organized school environment. One is safety, and the second is systematic and orderly procedures. We start with safety—creating a safe school environment. So how does one go about creating the ideal learning environment by beginning with safety? How does the principal create a school environment where every student feels, and is, safe? What needs to be done so that students know they can go to their locker, to the restroom, to the playground, or out on the campus without having to worry about being bullied, or assaulted, or having their possessions stolen?

We begin with the premise that creating a sense of family among and between faculty, staff, students, and parents—all stakeholders—is a high priority of principals who are student advocates. The Support for Texas Academic Renewal (STAR) Center looked at twenty-six schools where student achievement, as measured by the state's assessment of academic skills, was among the highest. They identified seven key attributes the schools had in common. One was a sense of family. The researchers observed a powerful sense of family, where statements such as "We're a family here," or "These are all my children," were heard frequently (Support for Texas Academic Renewal, 1997). School personnel saw their school more as a family and less as an institution.

In these schools, observers noted that students were treated with respect and concern. The actions of teachers, administrators, parents, and other members of the school community frequently reflected the concern, dedication, involvement, respect, and love that one would expect to find in the healthiest of families.

We contend that maintaining a safe school necessarily involves the principal and his or her staff's shared vision of what the school should be. This contention is supported by principals themselves. In one interview, a principal stated that even though things have changed in the almost twenty years he had been in the office, he still felt he still had an exciting opportunity to mold school culture. One of his teachers reported that it was the consensus of the faculty that this principal is a strong advocate for students. For example, one of the first things he did his first year was to take steps to create a positive and safe climate. His basic strategy and top priority was to promote a "family atmosphere" at the school. That philosophy continues to this day. The principal has implemented a number of strategies to create that atmosphere. One has been to hire staff members who are student centered and themselves advocates for students. Teacher interview and selection techniques are as focused on teacher-student relationships as on knowledge and experience.

Once he is satisfied that the knowledge and certification requirements are met, he probes deeply into the candidate's interpersonal and relationship-building skills, concern for students, and demonstrated history of serving students. Another strategy has been to encourage teachers to have their own children attend the school. As one teacher reported, "When you walk onto this campus, it does feel like a family." The principal has tried his very best to make all persons involved in the school—students, parents, teachers, faculty, and staff—feel like it is their home away from home. The principal stated that creating a "family atmosphere" would eventually lead to teachers taking the position that all the students at the school were "their" students.

Students recognize a principal who has their best interests at heart and is an advocate for them. Another opportunity to create a family atmosphere is the lunch period. Students told one teacher that their principal makes them feel special when he sits down at their table at lunch. He doesn't just stand at one end of the cafeteria or walk around and look at them. He will sit down at their table and talk with them about what they did over the weekend or what their plans are for the next break.

One student reported that the first time she walked on campus the principal asked her name, what school she had previously attended, and then asked her to tell him something about her family. The next day, the principal greeted her by name as she walked onto campus and asked how she was doing. The student reported that she will never forget how she was greeted and that she knows that the principal sincerely cares about her. Creating a family atmosphere includes taking a personal interest in students in a variety of situations throughout the school day.

One teacher related a conference she had with the principal following one of his observations of her teaching. He went through the usual summation of his observations and recommendations and then wound up to the effect of, "Enough of that. Now, I want to know about you—how are you doing? Are things OK?" The teacher was struck by this demonstration of the principal's sincere care and concern about her well-being as a person—a member of the school "family."

Teachers working from the standpoint that all the children at the school are their children foster an atmosphere of caring, concern, and respect. Respect for one another—teachers for teachers, students for students, teachers for students, and students for teachers—minimizes the disruptive behaviors that lead to fighting, bullying, verbal threats, or intimidation. The principal modeling a sincere concern for every single teacher and staff person on his or her campus encourages a culture where all individuals treat each other with respect and contributes significantly to a safe environment.

Constructing an Orderly School Environment

For Lezotte and McKee-Snyder (2011), a key characteristic of an effective school is an orderly, purposeful, and businesslike atmosphere. The principal who creates these conditions sets the stage for staff and students to function comfortably and safely. Consider all the operations requiring organization, systems, and procedure in your school: enrollment, registration and course selection, budgeting, guidance and counseling, health services, teacher evaluation, discipline, entering and leaving campus, athletics, courses of study, curriculum, parking, parent and booster clubs, extra- and cocurricular activities, special-interest clubs and organizations. Does it ever end? What are the expectations of parents, students, teachers, stakeholders? The following offers answers to such questions.

Characteristics of an Organized School

In an organized school, orderly and systematic processes lead to high expectations among and between patrons, faculty, staff, and administration. Lines of communication are clearly defined and followed. Procedures for students new to the school, such as registration, testing, and course selection, are established, understood by staff, and executed in a timely, efficient, and caring manner. When the question of how something gets done is asked, the procedures and responsible individuals are clearly identifiable, and well-known by students, faculty, staff, and parents. Figure 4.1 contains characteristics important to the organization of your school. We suggest that you first score the items for yourself then give the form to your faculty and staff. Compare your perceptions with theirs. Then develop a plan to address those characteristics where the largest gap exists between your perceptions and theirs.

Another characteristic is a well-maintained campus. An orderly environment extends to the physical condition of the campus; there should be no litter, vandalism, graffiti, or unkept areas. Buildings and rooms must be clearly identified and traffic patterns indicated and adhered to by all.

The first thing a person expects when he or she enters the front office is a prompt, friendly, and courteous greeting. As discussed in Chapter 3, the front-office contact is the first many parents and students have with the school. It is the front-office staff that makes the first impression on the parent and the student. As representatives of the principal and the school, it is imperative that front office personnel be friendly, courteous, and cheerful when visitors enter. It is important that they bear in mind always why they are there in the first place—for the student. They must remember to leave their personal problems and bad moods at home. The front office is not the place to be rude or curt with visitors. Everyone who walks into the office has an issue or problem that they feel the front office can resolve. An enthusiastic, friendly, helpful greeting will go a long way toward establishing a positive relationship with the visitor.

Organized procedures and tasks conducted in a systematic fashion solidify the impression of an orderly environment. Individuals who have business to conduct or issues to resolve want to know that when they interact with a person responsible for the issue or problem they are going to get an answer to their questions. Should that person not have answers at the moment, the individual must be able to expect timely answers. Reliability is an important characteristic of personnel in an organized school.

There is no substitute for knowledgeable staff. Regardless of the department or function, staff persons are expected to be knowledgeable about the services they provide. Any individual—teacher, staff member, student, or parent—must be considered a "customer" of the department. Other essentials include:

- courtesy at all times toward all individuals
- dependability and reliability when providing answers to questions or solutions to problems
- promptness when individuals arrive at the work station
- friendly, cheerful, and enthusiastic greetings at all times

FIGURE 4.1 Organizational Characteristics Self-Analysis

To what extent are the following characteristics evident in my school?

Characteristics	*Score:* *1 = low* *10 = high*
Operational standards, procedures, and routines are established and documented.	
All personnel follow specified processes in executing tasks.	
Duplicate tasks are eliminated wherever possible.	
All personnel perform their tasks right the first time.	
All personnel accept responsibility for performing their assigned tasks.	
All personnel commit to the highest quality of performance in all aspects of the job.	
Information sources are clearly identified and readily available to all personnel and stakeholders.	
Periodic in-service sessions are conducted with faculty and staff to improve job performance.	
Clear structures, rules, and procedures for students are provided and enforced.	

The Principal's Role in Creating an Orderly Environment

Can the principal do it all? No. We contend, however, that the principal can ensure that all responsible parties have clearly defined and established procedures and regulations guiding their actions. The principal can also set the performance bar high, in the expectation that all individuals know well their responsibilities and skillfully carry them out. Lezotte and McKee-Snyder (2011) note, "Optimal learning environments tend to be organized and relatively calm. When classrooms or schools are chaotic, even well-motivated learners struggle to maintain the focus demanded by the learning task" (p. 105). A well-organized school enables teachers to teach comfortably in an environment where the expectations are clearly known, where the procedures for conducting the business of the school are clearly identified, and where all personnel carry out their responsibilities in an efficient and systematic manner.

Orderliness, for example, may include the simple expectation of punctuality: everyone—faculty, staff, and students—will be on time to all scheduled events, including classes, faculty meetings, assemblies, and departmental meetings. Being late or tardy is not acceptable. The principal of one school communicated punctuality so effectively to his faculty and staff that they would rather miss a meeting than be late. His motto was, "Reward those who are on time—not those who are late." His meetings started on time and ended on time. That practice carried over to the classroom, where teachers began instruction on time. Tardies were practically nonexistent at that school.

Creating an orderly environment includes creating a systematic way to identify students who are falling behind academically and designing programs to enable them to reach the desired levels of achievement. One principal interviewed formed a "data team" at his school, which consists of the principal together with teachers representing their respective grade levels or disciplines. On a regular basis, the team systematically reviews and analyzes student performance data. Students not performing at expected levels are identified, and they are assigned to an appropriate tutorial or remedial program. These include pull-out situations during the school day, study groups at the end of the day, and study groups during school-break or recess times. Teachers serving on data teams become more attuned to the importance of collecting and analyzing data and identifying students in need of additional assistance. The importance of every student succeeding is emphasized and steps are taken to ensure that students are achieving academically. The uniqueness of this approach is that, rather than isolated teachers, a team of staff members analyzes the performance of all students. This strengthens the relationship between and among teachers, enhances their understanding of the unique characteristics of the different academic disciplines, and strengthens their commitment to all students' success.

Collaboration

Principals who create safe and orderly schools concentrate on the overall school culture and make sure that every teacher's classroom reflects the common vision of learning for all, respect, and collaboration. The principals who create situations for collaboration and collegiality among and between teachers and staff members are among the most successful in creating a safe and orderly environment (Lezotte and McKee-Snyder, 2011). For the principal, collaboration is a powerful tool. Of the hundreds of examples of collaboration in all types of businesses and organizations that appear in the literature, it can be said: "They show a profound shift in the way people think and operate in their professional lives—from being an individual who asks, "What can I create?" to being a collaborative person who asks, "What can we create together?" (Hargrove, 1998, p. 12).

Collaboration between and among teachers and staff members taps the knowledge, skills, and experiences of all who are involved. Hargrove (1998) writes, "We engage in collaborative conversations to accomplish something that we passionately care about" (p. 167). In a school environment where all persons advocate for all students, we expect all adults to care passionately about those students and commit to exhausting all resources to ensure a positive, rewarding, and successful school experience. Collaborative conversation is the principal's best tool for addressing problems in the school, identifying goals and objectives for the next school year, reviewing student achievement, developing plans to narrow achievement gaps, discussing strategies for school improvement, resolving the tardiness problem, breaking gang relationships on campus, or planning the faculty end-of-year social event. Being a member of a collaborative team results in commitment and loyalty to and enthusiasm for the decisions it makes. Membership also strengthens the "family" atmosphere and sense of belonging. Members of the team feel they are on the inside rather than on the outside looking in. For the principal, Huszczo (1996) suggests that collaborative teams (1) usually produce higher-quality solutions than individuals working independently; (2) provide a structure that encourages a sense of involvement; and (3) offer a means of satisfying relationship/belongingness needs and thus provide a sense of satisfaction. All staff members should be given an opportunity to be a member of a collaborative team at some time during the school year.

Collaboration contributes significantly to a positive organizational climate in which all faculty and staff participate in the success of the school. Ulrich, Zenger, and Smallwood (1999) state that organizational culture "provides a key link between a company [school] and its employees' motivation to do their best work, unleash their creativity, work with intensity, act with a sense of urgency, and put forth the extra effort when required" (p. 72). A culture of collaboration will motivate all staff to proceed as if they were on duty every day, all day, and all over the campus. When observing a student or students breaking a rule outside the classroom, rather than turn the other way and take the position that the inappropriate behavior is an administrator's responsibility, the teacher or staff member will take the initiative to stop the behavior, identify the student, and report the incident to the administration.

Creating Opportunities Through Faculty Collaboration

Providing students with a variety of opportunities to participate in school-connected activities is a must in an effective, family-oriented school. Much has been written about the benefits to students of extracurricular activities. Many will agree that students who participate in extracurricular activities learn teamwork, respect for each other, and respect for adults; make new friends; develop self-confidence; are more committed to improving their academic performance; and display better attitudes in classes. Student advocates will agree that there is no better way to develop self-esteem than by providing the opportunities for personal success that come through opportunities, whether in the classroom, on the athletic field, or in student clubs.

Collaboration between faculty and staff enables the principal to match student interests with those of faculty and staff and offer a variety of clubs and activities in which all feel engaged. One principal reported there were forty active clubs in his school, addressing a wide variety of student interests, including, for example: Running Club (described earlier in this chapter), Garden Club, Recycling Performance, Author's Teas, Climbing Club, Kindergarten Rodeo, Mousetrap Car Races, Thankful Tree Activity, Giving Tree Activity and Fine Dining. Each club was sponsored by a faculty or staff person, which added additional responsibilities to an already full assignment.

Dealing with Disruptive Behavior in a Safe and Orderly Environment

Setting precedent for a positive school climate at the beginning of the school year is an important task of the principal and faculty. One way this is accomplished is the distribution of the student-parent handbook during the first week of school. An entire class period is devoted to orienting the students to the handbook, discussing the expectations articulated there, and reviewing the more serious violations and the associated disciplinary actions. This orientation is presented by the classroom teacher. In those schools where closed-circuit television is available in all classrooms, the principal often conducts the orientation, using that medium. The principal who is a student advocate emphasizes the behavioral expectations of a good student and good citizen of the school.

The handbook clearly identifies those behaviors considered unacceptable and the penalties involved should the student violate the district or school rules. The consequences of these behaviors are clearly identified, and they might range from a conference between student, parent, and school official to suspension or expulsion. These, too, are discussed with the students during the presentation.

Each student is expected to take the handbook home and discuss it with his or her parents. The student is given a document with a title such as "Acknowledgement of Handbook Receipt" that contains a paragraph similar to the following: "I have received a copy of the XYZ School District's Student-Parent Handbook for the current school year and have taken the time to review and discuss the policies and procedures with my child. I have placed particular emphasis on the discipline guidelines, the District's weapon policy (Governing Board Policy XXXX) and the Electronics Information Services Agreement (Governing Board Policy YYYY)." There is a place for the parent's signature and the student's signature as well as the date. The document contains a statement such as this: "Please sign and date this page and return it to the teacher or the school office during the first week of school." The student is expected to return the document to his or her designated teacher.

The teacher is required to take all the documents to the office for placement in the student's cumulative folder. For students entering after the first day of school, the handbook is reviewed with the parent and the student at the time of registration and the acknowledgement document signed and left with the school at that time. This signed document becomes very important when dealing with more serious offenses that may lead to suspension or expulsion. It is evidence that the student was made aware of the behavioral expectations of the school and of the penalties should the student violate any of the rules, regulations, policies, or procedures. The procedures for the distribution and collection of these important documents are clearly established and meet an important obligation the school has to advise students and their parents of undesirable or unacceptable behaviors and the consequences should the student engage in them; they fulfill an important due-process requirement in the event of the suspension or expulsion of the student. The student-parent handbook also clearly advises students and parents on such matters as how and when to communicate with teachers, support staff, and the administration.

Regardless of how hard the principal and staff try to create an environment in which every student experiences school in a positive and rewarding manner, not every student follows all the rules or treats other students and teachers with respect. There are going to be occasions when a rule is broken, a policy violated, or a regulation ignored. Depending on the severity of the matter, it may be handled by a teacher, a dean, an assistant principal, or the principal. The student advocate will make every effort to ensure that the decision made, whether punitive or remedial, is in the best interests of the student and the school.

The principal must consider a number of factors when adjudicating a disciplinary issue. The first is whether the student was aware of the behavior expected of him or her. The second is whether the student was aware of the behaviors that constituted a violation of a school or district procedure, policy, or regulation and of the consequences of violation. One school district believes that a positive learning environment and good student conduct starts with students, parents, and staff having a thorough knowledge and understanding of the basic standards of acceptable conduct. The district has identified aggravating and mitigating factors that must be considered by the principal when addressing a disciplinary problem. Aggravating factors include:

- ◆ the severity of the actual result of the conduct
- ◆ the actual and potential jeopardy to the members of the educational community
- ◆ the extent of the actual and potential disruption to the educational environment
- ◆ the attitudes of student and parent concerning the misconduct and potential disciplinary consequences
- ◆ any previous pattern of misconduct, with or without disciplinary intervention
- ◆ whether the student's behavior violated civil or criminal law

Mitigating factors include:

- ◆ the age of the student
- ◆ the ability of the student to understand that the conduct was prohibited
- ◆ the ability of the student to understand the risk the misconduct posed to the health and safety of others and to their property
- ◆ the ability of the student to understand the potential disruption to the institution
- ◆ the ability of the student to understand the potential disciplinary consequences

- ◆ reasonableness of use of physical force in self-defense, defense of others, and defense of property
- ◆ frequency, type, and magnitude of previous misbehaviors by the student
- ◆ special intellectual, psychological, emotional, physical, or environmental characteristics of the student

Questions the Student Advocate Must Answer in Disciplinary Cases

Not all disciplinary problems are referred to the principal. For those that are, a number of questions surface with which the principal must grapple:

- ◆ What is this student's prior disciplinary history?
- ◆ Is this the first offense of this nature?
- ◆ What impact will the action taken in this instance have on the future education of this student?
- ◆ What disciplinary alternatives do I have in dealing with this case?
- ◆ What message will be conveyed to other students by the decision I make in this matter?
- ◆ Will the teacher(s) involved in the situation feel I have supported or abandoned them?
- ◆ Will my decision engender support from the teacher or teachers?
- ◆ To what extent did the student's behavior disrupt the normal educational processes at my school?
- ◆ Is my decision in the best interests of this student?
- ◆ To what extent must I consider the impact of the student's behavior in this matter on other students?

Given these and other questions that the principal may consider as disciplinary action is contemplated, we offer the following actual scenarios taken from principals' experience and ask you to carefully consider what action you would take or recommend in light of your commitment to student advocacy. Names and locations have been changed to protect the privacy of those involved. The principal's actions in each instance are included in the scenario.

Additionally, we present a variety of intervention strategies available to the principal at the time the case is discussed with the student. As you review the incident, we ask you to consider all the intervention possibilities and any prior behavioral issues and choose the strategy you feel most appropriate to the behavior exhibited by the student. The strategies include student referral to or conference with a school counselor or intervention specialist; a telephone call to the parent; student conference with the principal; parent-teacher conference; student-parent conference with the principal; report to the local police department; after-school detention; school-team threat assessment; on-campus suspension; off-campus suspension; expulsion.

Scenario 1

On February 3, Student A's teacher first reported difficulties she was having with Student A in her classroom. Student A rolled his eyes at the teacher in a disrespectful manner, called other students names, and was pushing other students around. The teacher referred the student to the principal. The principal met with Student A and counseled him.

On February 5, the principal received a bus referral indicating that Student A was using foul language on the bus and admitted calling another student a "b——h." The principal attempted to contact Student A's parents but was unable to do so.

On February 11, Student A was chased and called names by other students. The principal met with Student A and the other students.

On February 13, Student A was accidentally hit by a ball. Student A then spit on and tried to trip another student. During a conference with the principal following this incident, Student A reported having problems with his brother and sister at home and that they called him stupid. The principal called home and spoke with Student A's sister and requested that the parent call. No contact was made with the parent. At this point, the frequency (four offenses over a ten-day period) of Student A's violations of school policy warranted the involvement of a counselor or intervention specialist. The frequency would appear to be a clear indicator of a serious problems adjusting to the school. Whether or not another school professional is involved, a parent conference with the principal and the student would be in order—something the principal would strongly recommend before permitting the student back into regular classes. Additionally, the principal conferring with Student A's teacher or teachers would give them better insight into the issues Student A was having at school and aid determining the best course of action to assist him.

On February 15, Student A was reported for fighting on the playground, where he was showing extreme levels of anger. During the conference with the principal Student A reported that his brother and sister hit him at home and that when he uses bad language at home, his mother slaps him in the mouth. The principal spoke with Student A's mother, who expressed concern about his anger. Student A was suspended for five days for fighting. With this incident occurring only two days after a conference with the principal over spitting on another student, the student advocate would recognize the serious problems Student A was having adjusting to life at the school. The principal should demand a conference with the parent and confer with other members of the school staff. The principal might also suggest that the parent and Student A participate in behavior-management or anger-management classes offered by the district.

On February 18, Student A hit two first grade students on the bus. Student A lost bus privileges for five days, during which time he did not attend school. The principal spoke with Student A's mother, who again demonstrated concern about Student A's anger. Upon regaining bus privileges, Student A was assigned a seat in the front row of the bus and asked by the bus driver to be his helper. After a few weeks of helping the bus driver, Student A would often put his foot in the aisle, tripping other students.

On May 1, Student A was part of a group setting off stink bombs on the campus. Student A was suspended and lost the privilege to participate in a scheduled field trip. He was given the opportunity to earn the privilege back by exhibiting excellent behavior and community service. On May 18, Student A brought a BB gun to school, with the intent to use it at school. He was observed shooting other students while they got off the bus at an apartment complex.

On May 20, Student A was recommended for expulsion.

Consider the scenario just described and assume it occurred in your school. Take the position that you are going to be as strong a student advocate as you can be as you deal with each of the incidents. What resources or intervention options do you have available to deal with these kinds of situations? Would you have handled the situations differently? If so, how?

Scenario 2

Drug possession, use, sale, and distribution are an ever-increasing menace in many communities. Students as young as sixth-graders are being used to sell and distribute drugs on and around their campuses. Consider the following scenario.

On December 9, a teacher gave the principal a backpack that was found in the teacher's classroom. Inside the backpack, a strong odor of marijuana was detected and a switchblade knife, a tin containing marijuana, and drug paraphernalia were discovered. The owner of the backpack, Student B, was summoned to the office. Student B admitted bringing the container of marijuana to school along with the switchblade knife. Student B claimed he was holding the items for another student. Student B admitted to smoking marijuana on the way to school that morning.

Student B has been a student at this school for one and one-half years and has been involved in minor incidents since entering the school. After considering the nature of the infractions, the principal recommended that rather than be suspended Student B be assigned to the district's alternative-education program through the end of the current school year. The principal, a student advocate, recognized that placement in the alternative program afforded the student the opportunity to continue his education and, with continued good conduct, be admitted to the regular school program at the beginning of the following school year.

In this instance, a drug violation is defined as use, possession, sale, or being under the influence of drugs on school property or at school events. The consequences for violating the district's policy include conference, detention, suspension, expulsion, police report, and "other." "Other" is not clearly defined. Further, the district has identified three levels of behavioral offense: Level I: Serious; Level II: Severe; and Level III: Extreme. Drug violations as defined above are considered a Level III offense.

Again, consider the scenario just described and assume it occurred in your school. Take the position that you are going to be as strong a student advocate as you can be as you deal with the student's behavior. What resources or intervention options do you have available to deal with these kinds of situations? Would you have handled the situation differently? If so, how?

The principal who is a committed advocate for students considers all the available intervention and prevention resources in each disciplinary case he or she addresses. In a well-organized school, the principal has made the faculty and staff aware of such resources and encourages staff to utilize them in all appropriate instances. The principal who is an advocate for students will expect the teacher to exhaust all the school's available resources prior to referring the matter to the administration.

Recommending Long-Term Suspension or Expulsion

Long-term suspension and expulsion represent the most serious action a principal can recommend when dealing with students whose behaviors violate a school or district rule, regulation, policy, or procedure.

Before making a recommendation for long-term suspension or expulsion, student advocates make use of every available resource in the attempt to improve the student's behavior: conferences with the parent; referrals to other staff for intervention; detention; on-campus suspension; and placement in an alternative educational program. All are considered—all with the best interests of the student in mind.

Due Process for Students in Disciplinary Hearings

Due process is guaranteed to every citizen of the United States by the Fourteenth Amendment to the Constitution. Due process is best defined as fairness. Before taking the rights away from any student, school officials must provide fair procedures or due process for that student. In matters of serious student disciplinary violations, an unbiased hearing that follows fair and just procedures is commonly arranged. We submit that a due process hearing is a primary provision for ensuring that a student's rights are protected.

It is beyond the scope of this chapter to detail the rather complex considerations of all requirements involved in the preparation, implementation, and reporting of student disciplinary hearings. However, many of the important factors that serve in advocating student rights are outlined in the following information and the special roles of the school principal are discussed.

Procedural due process centers on fairness; how the law is just. For example, is the law, policy, or regulation too vague? Is it applied fairly? Does it presume guilt? Substantive due process centers on why the law is just in regard to fundamental rights. It considers the reasonableness of the law.

Due process usually advocates for students by guaranteeing provisions that include the following:

- notice of charges
- right to be present when adverse evidence is presented
- opportunity to rebut charges in a fair and just proceeding with a neutral and impartial hearing officer
- right to present witnesses on one's behalf
- right to be heard in one's own defense
- right to counsel
- right to cross-examine witnesses

Advocate Role of the School Principal

The role of the school principal as it relates to student disciplinary hearing is derived primarily from three sources: state law, governing board policy and/or regulations, and the student conduct handbook. If the severity of the student's offense results in the principal recommending expulsion, then state laws commonly dictate that: (1) the governing school board of the district be notified of the intended action and (2) the governing board in executive session decides whether or not to hold a hearing or to have a hearing officer hold the hearing to receive evidence, prepare a record of the hearing, and to bring a recommendation to the board for action. In most cases, the principal's role is to serve as a witness when the case is presented and be certain that the information presented by the school officials is accurate, documented, and fair. Have the student's rights been properly represented? Has the student been afforded necessary and competent counsel? Have the student's parents or guardians been properly informed of the accusations, the school regulations that have been allegedly violated, and the rights of the student in such matter?

The advocate principal makes certain that he or she is thoroughly prepared for the hearing. The size of the school and its number of administrators commonly determines whether the school principal or another administrator or faculty member will assume the responsibility for investigating a particular disciplinary matter. In any case, it is the school principal who is responsible for overseeing the case and ensuring that the evidence presented at the hearing is accurate.

The school principal who recommends that a student be subjected to a suspension or expulsion has exhausted all the resources at his or her disposal in order to help the student make better decisions relative to future behavior. Committing to advocating for students in disciplinary cases will minimize the need to recommend students for more serious punishment; other alternatives are more likely to result in positive learning for the student and support rather than inhibit future positive behavior.

Summary

This chapter emphasized the importance of creating a favorable environment for teachers to teach and students to learn. We pointed out that this environment must be one that is safe and orderly. We noted that these two conditions must constitute a high priority for the principal who desires to become an even stronger advocate for students. We emphasized the importance of a well-organized school in which personnel and offices function in a systematic and efficient manner. Collaboration between and among faculty, staff, and administration is an important tool for building collegiality, enhancing a team approach to student issues, and arriving at the best solutions to which all parties are fully committed. We discussed the benefits of creating a school with a family atmosphere, along with strategies the principal can use to create such an atmosphere.

Application Exercises

Application Exercise 1 (Adapted from Lezotte, 2002.)

Take the following statement and complete the related activities:

My school has made a long-term commitment to becoming a school known for its advocacy for all students.

1. Individually, list all the pluses or positives this statement suggests.
2. Individually, list all the negatives or minuses this statement suggests.
3. In small groups, discuss the positives and negatives identified by those in your group and identify common issues or questions.
4. In small groups, discuss what each staff member can do to more effectively and efficiently advocate for all students.
5. In small groups, identify attitudinal changes that need to be made or attitudinal "slogans" that need to be internalized and practiced.

Application Exercise 2

On a scale of one to five, rate your agreement or disagreement with each of the indicators of safe school environments at your school (Figure 4.2, page 92).

In small groups, determine those factors that need additional attention and design and implement strategies to address them. New indicators may certainly be added during the course of the school year as they are identified. This is a tool for what should become your school's on-going self-evaluation of its safe and orderly environment for teaching and learning.

FIGURE 4.2 Assessment of a Safe Environment

Disagree Strongly				Agree Strongly
1	2	3	4	5

Indicators of a Safe School Environment	Rating
Routine discipline problems are declining/minimized.	
Severe discipline problems are declining/minimized.	
Appropriate behaviors are recognized, reinforced, and rewarded.	
Incidents of littering, graffiti, and other forms of vandalism are declining.	
Students are notified of unacceptable behaviors and their consequences.	
Responses to disciplinary problems are timely and appropriate.	

5

Principal Student Advocacy and the Student with Disabilities

Let's Set the Stage, With You in the Lead Role

Our contention in each of the foregoing chapters has been that student advocacy is important for meeting the educational needs of all students, not only children with special needs. Student advocacy begins with the principal's desire to create a school inclusive in the broadest sense. But you only have to review the literature or mention in professional company the topic of student advocacy to be reminded that it is commonly associated with special education. We certainly agree that the student advocacy concept is of paramount importance in the education of students with disabilities. Our focus in this chapter is student advocacy as it affects the success of special-education programs and the welfare of students with disabilities in schools.

We begin by reviewing the status of special-education programs in schools today and examine some of the legal mandates that determine the administration of the special-education program. After this, we ask: "How do principal student advocates assure viable special-education programs for disabled students?" "What distinct administrative competencies relative to the administration of special-education programs do principal student advocates possess?" We conclude with "snapshots" of principal student advocates working successfully in programs with students with disabilities.

Both research and empirical evidence suggest that school principals commonly are not adequately prepared to oversee the special-education programs in their schools. Cooner, Tochterman, and Garrison-Wade (2005-2006) report that educational leadership is ranked as the key variable associated with school effectiveness, but the principal must be a leader for all programs within the school, special education not excepted. There is sufficient evidence to support the contention that the attitude and leadership of the school principal are essential for the administration of effective special-education programs and for the development of school-district policies and regulations and school rules beneficial to students with disabilities (Evans et al., 1992; McAnely, 1992; Guzman & Schofield, 1995; Praisner, 2003). Lavoie (2010) makes the point explicitly:

> No matter how talented or devoted the faculty is, no matter how powerful or influential the parent body is, no matter how committed the School Board is . . . the child will NOT get responsible effective services unless he has the support of the person in the principal's office. (p. 6)

How much of your workday do you believe that you spend on matters related to special education? Empirical evidence suggests that special-education programs and activities on average consume 30 percent of the school principal's total work time.

Did you know that over six million school children ages six to twenty-one are receiving special education services in schools today (American Youth Policy Forum, 2002) and that 67 percent of these have specific learning disabilities or speech and language impairments? About 12 percent are children with cognitive disabilities such as mental retardation or traumatic brain injury. The large majority of these pupils spend school time with other pupils in regular classrooms. As you most likely are aware, the implications of these numbers for the work of the school principal are far reaching.

In this chapter, you will examine briefly the responsibilities of school principals for meeting the special education requirements of students as set forth in state and federal laws and local school policies and regulations. We will also review the advocacy behaviors that accompany effective programs. But before we move on we ask you once again to assess your knowledge of certain features of special-education administration, with a focus on Section 504 of the Rehabilitation Act of 1973. Again, no one else will see your assessment results. Each question posed suggests a topic of interest that will be discussed in the following sections of the chapter.

True or False?

_____ 1. Section 504 of the Rehabilitation Act of 1973, civil-rights statute that requires the needs of students with disabilities to be met as adequately as the needs of the nondisabled are met.

_____ 2. Studies have shown that principals with no previous special-education experience rated themselves as providing greater administrative support to special-education teachers than principals with previous special-education experience.

_____ 3. Section 504 of the Rehabilitation Act does not exclude students who are users of alcohol.

_____ 4. Discipline of a child with a disability must take that disability into account.

_____ 5. Public-school districts are responsible for identifying all students with disabilities within their jurisdictions, regardless of whether they are attending public schools, since private institutions may not be funded for providing accommodations under IDEA (Individuals with Disabilities Education Act, 1990).

_____ 6. IDEA applies only to those states and their local educational agencies that accept federal funding under IDEA.

_____ 7. Conditions or disorders such as diabetes, epilepsy, allergies, low vision, poor hearing, heart disease, and chronic illness may not be obvious, but if they substantially limit students' ability to receive an appropriate education, then students afflicted with them may be considered to have impairments and qualify for benefits as disabled students.

_____ 8. FAPE stands for "Free and Appropriate Public Education."

_____ 9. Studies have overwhelmingly reported that 50 to 75 percent of the responsibility for the supervision and evaluation of special-education programs falls to local school principals.

_____ 10. A principal has to exercise caution when suspending students with special needs, because the courts place the burden of proof on the school in determining if the behavior was the result of the student's disability.

Check Your Results

Did you answer True to each of the ten statements? If so, consider yourself well informed about several important issues concerning special education and the disabled student. Which of the ten statements, if any, do you believe concern matters outside the immediate jurisdiction or administration of the school principal?

How Far We Have Come as Advocates for Students with Disabilities

In 1962 the Salina, Kansas, school district initiated its very first self-contained class for students with disabilities. A person who had been serving as a substitute teacher in the district was assigned as the special-education teacher for the class. The teacher had no preparation in special education and no specialists were available for support. The organizational arrangement for the special-education students was more a sheltered workshop than an individualized education program. Although nationally by 1962 some school districts were making progress in special education, the large majority of school districts were not including all eligible children in their public schools' special-education programs and activities.

Before the enactment of the Education for All Handicapped Children Act (EAHCA) in 1975, only 20 percent of children with disabilities were being educated by public schools in the United States. In 1975, some states still had laws that excluded children with certain disabilities from attending public school. The National Council on Disability reported that before EAHCA was enacted, more than one million children in the United States had no access to the public-school system. These disabled children were in state institutions or segregated facilities where they received limited educational services. According to the National Center for Disabilities, as of 2006, IDEA was providing special-education services for more than six million disabled children. We think you will agree that we have come a long way in providing educational opportunities for all children in our public schools in the United States.

The Many Special-Education Programs and Activities in Schools

The number of programs and special services provided for special-education students in schools today is practically limitless. Figure 5.1 lists some of the programs and services presently provided for special-education students. Services extend from those addressing speech and language pathologies to

FIGURE 5.1 Selected Student Disabilities and Services

Student Disabilities	*Student Special Services*
Physically Disabled Attention Deficit Disorder Neurological Impairments Serious Emotional Disturbances Speech and Language Impairments Orthopedic Impairments Autism/Pervasive Development Disorder Asperger's Syndrome Bipolar Disorder Blind and Visual Impairment Cerebral Palsy Chronic Health Problems Deaf and Hearing Impairment Mental Retardation Dyslexia Economic Disadvantaged Traumatic Brain Injury Homelessness Multi-Handicapped Student Learning Disabilities Learning Disabled/Gifted Student Tourette Syndrome	Evaluation and Referral Services Mobility Services Home and Hospital Services Occupational Therapy Parent Counseling/Training Psychological Services Referral Services Rehabilitation Counseling Social Work Services Therapeutic Recreation Medical Services for Diagnostic Purposes Home Schooling

psychological services; physical and orthopedic therapies; medical services for diagnostic purposes; education for the mentally retarded, the autistic, and those with other learning disabilities; programs for students with vision or hearing impairments, serious emotional problems, or brain injury; and on and on. In addition, principals need be concerned with all the administrative responsibilities associated with special education, such as staff development, counseling services, home and hospital educational services, school health services, parent counseling and training, child-find systems, student rights, and so on.

One student often overlooked is the learning disabled/gifted (LD/G) student (Norton, Hartwell-Hunnicutt, & Norton, 1996). Such students commonly display strengths in one area and severe weaknesses or disabilities in others. A difficulty in working with LD/G students is their ability to "cover up" or compensate for their disabilities.

Collaboration in the planning and implementation of special-education programs and activities is, of course, imperative. Special-education specialists, guidance counselors, school nurses, social workers, the special-education staff, central-office personnel, regular classroom teachers, and many other school personnel carry out the services or support them in numerous ways. Direct participation in special-education programs and activities by the school principal demonstrates personal interest and allows for direct insight into the accomplishments and the problems and needs of the programs.

Planning, Organizing, Implementing, and Evaluating Procedures

The planning, organizing, implementing, and evaluating procedures for special education are ongoing responsibilities of the school principal. They typically include the following:

1. Search and Find Procedures

Principals are required by law to find all disabled children in their school district and report their findings to the proper authorities. The search and find requirement applies whether or not the disabled child is a potential enrollee in the principal's school.

2. Screening Procedures

Educational and health screenings are ongoing responsibilities of teachers, the school principal, guidance counselors, nurses, special-education personnel, and other members of the staff. Early identification of disabled students and assessment of their needs are their responsibilities as well. Attendance, test data, student behavior, learning problems, social relationships, and other such matters are often indicators of a student with special needs.

3. Review-Team Procedures

A select support team is commonly organized to review cases of probable student disability. Such reviews can lead to a variety of referral recommendations, or they might include specific assessments of the student's condition and qualifications for a special-education program. Other special teams, consisting of the school principal, qualified special-education personnel, guidance counselors, and parents, are organized to review all of the assessment data and develop an appropriate instructional program for the disabled student. An Individualized Educational Program (IEP) is developed, an individually designed instruction plan for the student with disabilities. Special education is thus not a placement concept but an instructional one, specifying the modifications to content, instructional methods, and measures of achievement necessary to include the student in the general curriculum of the school. The IEP looms important in assessments of the student's progress, in disciplinary procedures, and in any matters that might be referred to or become the concern of the courts.

4. Implementation of the IEP

The educational program for the student is activated. All options for curricular programs, extracurricular activities, and individualization instruction are considered and the specifics implemented, as recommended by the IEP team. Instructional methods are selected so as to provide for the least-restricted environment. The principal is responsible for making certain that all those responsible for services ensure that the student's IEP goals are aligned with the school's general curriculum. Parents will sometimes challenge the appropriateness of their child's instructional services. The courts have ruled that the test for specially designed instruction services rests with this question: "Are the instructional program and other educational activities providing opportunities for adequate progress on the student's IEP?" That is, if the student has been making acceptable progress in the present instructional program, the courts have upheld the "stay-put" provision. Principal student advocates and other advocates for students with disabilities are essential for supporting students in cases in which parents do not assume their responsibilities for the child's welfare, deny that their child is disabled, or become unreasonable in their demands concerning the education of their child. In such cases, the student is in dire need of a caring advocate who can speak in his or her behalf.

Advocating for Special-Needs Students Through Policy Implementation

There are many reasons why school principals need to be knowledgeable of federal and state laws as well as school-district policy concerning special-education programs. Keeping the school in line with the law is one, but another is that the legislation consistently advocates for the disabled child. When the school principal knows and implements Section 504 of the Rehabilitation Act of 1973, for example, he or she is automatically initiating student advocacy principles relative to the instructional program, student discipline, student placement, inclusion, extracurricular activities, student rights, parent rights, and other program provisions. One school principal noted a difference between principal student advocates and others. Non-advocates *have* to implement the supporting laws; advocates *want* to implement them.

In the following section, we examine legislation that pertains to disabled students and therefore to special education. Keep in mind that our primary purpose is to illustrate how the implementation of the Individuals with Disabilities Education Act (IDEA) has advocated positively for the disabled student. A presentation of all legislation that has influenced special education practices in public schools is beyond the scope of this chapter. However, the Rehabilitation Act of 1973, the Education for All Handicapped Children Act of 1975, and IDEA are of paramount importance and so are summarized here.

The Rehabilitation Act of 1973–Section 504

Section 504 of the Rehabilitation Act states:

> No otherwise qualified individual with a disability in the United States . . . shall, solely by reason of his or her disability, be excluded from the participation in, be denied the benefits of, or be subjected to discrimination under any program or activity receiving Federal financial assistance or under any program or activity conducted by any Executive agency or by the United States Postal Service.

As applied to K–12 schools, Section 504 prohibits the denial of participation in public education or enjoyment of the benefits of public school programs because of a child's disability. School programs that take place outside of the regular school day, such as athletics, intramural sports, school clubs, handcrafts, school plays, and other extracurricular activities fall within the disabled student's rights of participation.

For example, assume that your industrial-arts teacher refused to accept a child with a physical disability. This rejection would be considered unjust under Section 504 unless school administrators and the teacher could provide evidence that the student's participation in the class would jeopardize the safety of the student or other students in the class. In such cases the law might require a written accommodation plan that would permit the student to participate in the class under specified arrangements, including special safety measures. Neither can a student be prohibited from participating in the school's glee club because he or she uses a wheelchair, nor be prohibited from participating on athletic teams because of a disability. Section 504 advocates for the student in such cases and protects the student from unjust treatment.

The Education for All Handicapped Children Act of 1975

The Education for All Handicapped Children Act of 1975 (EHA) advocates for the disabled student by removing discrimination of children with disability and assuring their participation in the educational programs and services that are enjoyed by other students. In 1986, amendments were added to the EHA that included preschool and infant-toddler program provisions. Later, in 1990, amendments were added, and the legislation was renamed the Individuals with Disabilities Education Act (IDEA). One amendment advocates for the disabled student in terms of program placement. Each student is to be educated in the least restrictive environment (LRE), to the maximum extent allowing for the student to progress, to be educated alongside children without disabilities, and to be educated in the same class as he or she would have been without the disability.

Individuals with Disabilities Education Act (IDEA), Enacted in 1990

IDEA was enacted to ensure that all students with disabilities have an opportunity to participate in a free, appropriate public education, one that emphasizes special education and other services to serve their particular needs. In addition, the law requires that each student be placed in programs and activities that:

- ◆ are appropriate to his or her continued progress in the general curriculum
- ◆ serve to meet predetermined goals
- ◆ provide for the special-education services necessary for the student to meet stated goals
- ◆ reveal the extent to which the student participates in the learning process with nondisabled students
- ◆ include appropriate methods of assessment of the student's progress

The disabled student's school program is individualized through the use of an IEP that must result in student achievement. IDEA advocates for the student in many ways and guarantees that the disabled student will have the same opportunities in the educational program that all other students in the school enjoy. When school principals take the lead in implementing the provisions of IDEA, they are implementing the principles of student advocacy as well. The knowledge, skills, attitudes, and beliefs that school principals possess concerning special education are of paramount importance to the program's overall effectiveness.

Although school principals who are administering special-education programs are required to implement laws that of themselves do advocate for students with disabilities, this fact does not guarantee that the school principal is a strong student advocate.

How the School Principal Serves as Student Advocate in Special-Education Programs

We have emphasized that school principals who are knowledgeable of the laws concerning special education are already advocating for the program. You might ask, "But aren't all school principals advocates for special education programs?" Research suggests that, unfortunately, few school leaders are well prepared for this responsibility. It is clear that the primary requirements for student advocacy on the part of principals are knowledge of the school's responsibilities as set forth in law and competence in implementing the legal mandates. In the following section, we discuss other traits, behaviors, knowledge, and skills that are demonstrated in practice by school principals who are advocates for special-education students.

Advocates Support Special Education

There is sufficient evidence to conclude that principal student advocates are proactive in their support of special education, hold high expectations for disabled students, encourage program interventions that promote learning opportunities for all students, and focus on positive outcomes for all—students with disabilities, at-risk students, and nondisabled students.

Principal student advocates invest the time necessary to implement the inclusion requirements of federal and state laws. They work diligently to gain the adoption of policies and regulations that support the needs and interests of students with disabilities. They focus on what the student with disabilities can do rather than what they cannot do. They work to change or nullify policies and regulations that are not in the best interests of all students. They communicate and work cooperatively with special-education teachers, counselors, regular classroom teachers, itinerant staff, parents, and special-education personnel in district's central offices to fulfill the school's needs relative to quality programs for children with disabilities.

Advocates Practice Continuous Self-Development

Principal advocates of special education give due attention to increasing their own knowledge and skills relative to special education and student disabilities in order to administer programs more effectively. Advocates have a research posture of dissemination and implementation of quality research best practices in effective special-education programs. A research posture puts the principal in a better position to improve the understanding of others and so gain their support for implementing best practices in the special-education program. For example, knowledge of research findings regarding student retention, team building, nonpunitive discipline, mainstreaming, instruction for nonverbal learners, and other educational provisions give the principal a foundation for advocacy when these matters arise.

Advocates Practice Collaboration

As noted in Chapter 2, student advocates are aware that collaboration and team building result in increased opportunities for fostering success in inclusive classrooms. Communication and cooperative efforts on the part of the principal, counselors, nurses, teachers, parents, and others result in an improved school climate that facilitates the success of special-education programs. A lack of administrative support is often cited as the reason for unsuccessful special-education programs and the failure to retain quality personnel. Burrello and Lashley (1992) and other authorities have emphasized that school principals must be stewards and coaches in the development of a culture of inclusiveness. Special-education student advocates possess several common characteristics (Guzman, 1997), including:

- ◆ their ability to establish a highly effective communication system among school personnel and other stakeholders
- ◆ their active participation in the development of students' IEPs

- ◆ their active involvement with the parents of students with disabilities
- ◆ their collaboration with others in the development of mission statements and explicit objectives relative to special education and inclusiveness
- ◆ their design and communication of clear policies and regulations relative to student discipline
- ◆ their provision of effective professional development activities that emphasize inclusiveness
- ◆ their effective skills in problem solving that include data gathering and analysis

How to Recognize a Principal Special-Education Advocate

Manus (1992) sets forth several ways in which visionary leadership can be identified. His criteria are so insightful that we have adapted them to the principles of student advocates. After Manus's concept of visionary leadership, then, we contend that principal student advocates of special education can be recognized by:

- ◆ how they honor and make commitments to special education and students with disabilities
- ◆ what they express interest in and what questions they ask about special education and students with disabilities
- ◆ where they choose to go and how they spend time with special education and students with disabilities
- ◆ when they choose to act and how they make their actions known relative to special education and students with disabilities
- ◆ how they organize their staff and the physical surroundings that are involved with special education and students with disabilities

We would add also, by (1) where they show courage in the support of a student with disabilities and stand against administrative actions that threaten his or her best interests; and (2) how they manifest a record of placing students with special needs in least restrictive and vigorous classes and programs.

During our interviews with school principals and others, we were touched by the many times they confessed feelings of defeat when they could not or did not meet the needs of the student with disabilities. Principal student advocates, like all other school administrators, are not always successful in their strategies to help students. Nevertheless, as was often said during our interviews, they "just keep on trying."

The Effective Principal Student Advocate and Competency-Based Administration

One way to assess your status as a principal student advocate is to examine the important tasks, competencies, and indicators of competency that relate to the administration of the special-education program. A *task* is viewed as a specific administrative responsibility, obligation, or requirement. Each task is accompanied by *competencies*, or abilities that must be implemented to accomplish the task. The principal's behaviors or the outcomes that illustrate his or hers ability to perform competently are termed *indicators of competency* (Norton, 2008).

School principals are well aware that with their position comes numerous major tasks and that each task necessitates the application of special competencies. Following are examples of competencies possessed by principal student advocates of special education. Note that each competency reveals a specific skill or ability that the principal must implement to accomplish the task . Principals also must acquire competencies in unifying the general-education and special-education programs.

Select Special-Education Competencies of School Principals

1. the ability to provide incentives and motivation to all staff members to engage in quality staff-development activities related to special education
2. the ability to develop, share, and implement the school's mission statement and promote its goals and objectives
3. the ability to develop communication and decision-making processes that foster team building among staff personnel and encourage them to share ideas for improving the special education program
4. the ability to participate with the IEP team to provide information about special education and related services that meet the individual needs and interests of the student
5. the ability to ensure that both special-education and general-curriculum teachers assume responsibility for the continuous progress of students with disabilities

6.   the ability to administer student discipline in accordance with the requirements of IDEA and the concepts related to nonpunitive discipline

7.   the ability to work cooperatively with special-education personnel in securing the necessary support and instructional materials for students, so that students have access to the general curriculum

8.   the ability to ensure that the diverse needs of students with disabilities are addressed in administrative and program decisions concerning curriculum and instruction, extracurricular activities, professional development, student assessment, and student services

9.   the ability to foster shared leadership to support new instructional initiatives and program changes that lead to improvements in the school's special-education program

10.   the ability to initiate strategies and relationships that foster a healthy school climate, one that encourages respect and promotes trust among staff members, students, and parents

11.   the ability to develop a plan for a comprehensive child-find system, so that all children in the school district who are in the need of special-education services are located, identified, and referred

12.   the ability to provide all students with disabilities access to all school programs, including the general curriculum, extracurricular activities, counseling services, health services, special-interest clubs, and other nonacademic services

13.   the ability to develop a master schedule that includes time for collaboration among staff personnel, establishes effective communication systems, and provides a high quality of service to special-education students and their parents

14.   the ability to demonstrate that the school is instituting programs and services to meet the requirements of special-education laws and policies

15.   the ability to protect the rights of students with disabilities and advocate for them by serving as an intercessor on their behalf

16.   the ability to acquire foundational knowledge and skills in special education to ensure that program decisions and student placement regarding special education are legally correct

17.   the ability to create a school climate in which students' special needs are recognized and equitably met

The challenge for the school principal is to develop the overt behaviors or indicators of competency that demonstrate that each competency is being practiced.

Now let's use two of the competencies from the above list and consider the indicators of competency that would show that they were being implemented. Figure 5.2 shows the two selected competencies (numbers 1 and 2) and several indicators of competency for each.

FIGURE 5.2 Indicators of Competency

1. The ability to provide incentives and motivation to all staff members to engage in quality staff-development activities related to special education.

Indicators of Competency
♦ The principal provides release time to staff to attend special-education conferences, meet with special-education personnel, observe colleagues' classrooms, and engage in independent research on special education.
♦ The principal encourages staff to join state and national professional associations concerned with special education.
♦ The principal provides time for all instructional personnel, education specialists, counselors, and parents to participate actively in special-education development.
♦ The principal ensures that professional-development programs and activities are in concert with the school's stated mission, especially as regards objectives for special education and the needs of students with disabilities.
♦ The principal makes certain that professional-development activities in special education are directly applicable to practice.

2. The ability to develop, share, and implement the school's mission statement and promote its goals and objectives.

Indicators of Competency
♦ The school's staff members, including the special-education instructional personnel, actively participate in the development and implementation of the school's mission statement.
♦ The school principal uses several methods to assure that the school's special-education goals and objectives are aligned with the school's mission and that continuous effort is made to realize them.
♦ The principal meets with the special-education staff, parents of children with disabilities, other members of the professional and support staffs, and students to stress the importance of the mission statement and to answer any questions regarding it.
♦ The school principal establishes clear and open channels of communication between his or her office, special-education staff, parents, students, and other stakeholders regarding all matters pertaining to special education.
♦ The school's mission statement encourages respect not only for students' disabilities but also for the culture and ethnic background.

Snapshots of Student Advocacy in Practice

In this final section, we document the implementation of student advocacy as revealed in the contemporary practices of several schools. In selecting these examples, we examined best practices as reported by schools, we examined the literature, and we contacted teachers, special-education personnel, school principals, school superintendents, and students regarding their relationships with special-education programs and with students with disabilities. The snapshots focus primarily on the school principal's advocacy for a single disabled child. However, others tell of student advocacy on the part of teachers, with the principal serving as an advocate for the teacher. Others point out significant research findings. The snapshots are not intended to describe the features of a quality special-education program; rather they show the behaviors of caring school principals as they work to support the special needs and interests of a student with disabilities. They tell of happenings, program interventions, initiatives to change staff behavior, and other actions that have led to improved programs for students with disabilities. Some snapshots offer relatively simple stories and others more complicated. Most of the stories are ongoing. That is, the student is still being served by the school's special-education program. Some snapshots will be applicable to your school setting and others not. Perhaps, however, each will provoke new thinking about what can be achieved for students with disabilities. Although each snapshot is a true report of an advocate's caring efforts, the names are fictitious, as you will understand. At the close of the chapter, you will be asked to think about an experience in special education that you view as a snapshot of your own student advocacy in practice.

Snapshot 1: A speech/language advocate gains the support of the school principal and capitalizes on the disabled student's personal interests to gain his motivation for learning.

This is a snapshot of a student with disabilities in speech/language and learning. The student's speech/language therapist was genuinely concerned about the student's prospects for success in a regular classroom. She asked for and gained the school principal's full support for extending her activities with the student. She had the student take an interest inventory and learned that the student was deeply interested in low-rider cars. The therapist capitalized on this interest to help the student become engaged in learning activities. She bought low-rider magazines for the student to read and brought films on building of low-rider cars for the student to watch. The therapist used these aids to practice language and to engage the student in vocabulary-building and reading-skills exercises. The academic activities were tied closely to the standards for the regular classroom.

The therapist reported considerable growth in the student's writing and verbal skills and in overall academic achievement. The low-rider magazine was given to the student as a reward for his progress and his success in the regular classroom. The speech-therapist advocate understood the importance of motivating students for learning through their personal interests, thereby helping them be successful in school and gain self-respect.

Snapshot 2: Ensuring academic and behavioral interventions for students with disabilities.

This chapter has underlined the importance of the school principal ensuring the implementation of academic and behavioral interventions for students with disabilities. Best practices have been suggested for monitoring implementation. For example, principals report that walkthrough classroom visitations have proven to be effective and expedient ways to observe how implementation is proceeding. Clinical supervision strategies also are used to help teachers plan academic interventions. Some principals mentioned the use of master teachers for demonstrating methods of implementation. Supervision strategies including performance evaluation, small-group think tanks, team building, and focus groups capitalize on idea sharing and demonstrating successful methods for tying academic objectives to classroom instruction.

Snapshot 3: The principal serves as a model for acceptance of all students.

Most everyone would agree that the school principal's attitude and administrative behavior relative to special education programs are critical to the program's success. Along with competence regarding the application of the laws and policies that guide special-education programs and services, school principals point to the importance of visiting classrooms daily and spending time with students with disabilities. Principal student advocates frequently recall occasions in which they stood and vocally supported decisions and policies that would improve program services for students with disabilities or stood and challenged actions that would have resulted in inhibiting best practices.

The principal must provide evidence that the achievement gap is being closed and embrace areas in which the school is being held accountable. For example, principal and faculty could focus on students' IEP plans and demonstrate how for each student learning activities and experiences are tied to the IEP goals. A record of testing and assessment results could be presented that reveals evidence of progress. In cases where progress is not evident, it could be shown that adjustments to the learning strategies for the student have been implemented. Where progress is clear, evidence that the methods in place were reinforced might be presented. In serving as a role model for others, principal student advocates tend to ask the question, "Is this decision or program in the best interest of students or is it more in the vested interests of teachers and administrators?"

Snapshot 4: Advocating for students through conflict resolution and personnel collaboration.

Broughton (2005) points out that effective collaboration between school principals and counselors results in better programs and services for students. Research has demonstrated that when it comes to students with disabilities principals and counselors have differing perspectives on such issues such as student discipline, confidentiality, professional responsibilities, and parental involvement. Broughton supports the contention that principals and counselors can learn to understand and appreciate their differing roles and responsibilities. Through small-group discussions (focus groups) they can air their expectations and experiences regarding relationships between the two roles and the areas in which they have worked well and not so well together. Responses can be synthesized and analyzed to identify collaborative initiatives in the best interests of students. There could be a collaborative effort, for example, toward transitioning students with special needs into learning experiences or outreach programs that ensure independent living and the ability to make positive contributions as they become adults.

Such focus sessions open the door to better understanding and appreciation of the responsibilities of the two roles. Several best practices for establishing close working relationships were recommended by Broughton (2005):

◆ Principals and counselors should meet routinely, not just in times of crisis.

◆ Principals and counselors can build and sustain trust through the development of an understanding of their respective roles; collaborative settings for problem solving in such matters as student discipline and inclusion lead to better student-advocacy practices.

◆ Principals and counselors should establish clear procedures and protocols for handling student issues, sharing information, discussing disciplinary alternatives, and deciding on special services for students.

◆ The school principal should advocate for the counselor's role in support of students with disabilities.

Snapshot 5: How to integrate the special-education student into physical education.

A best-practices article by Sue Watson (2008), "How to Integrate the Special Education Needs Student into Physical Education," is so unique and relevant to the principles of student advocacy that we wanted to share it in this section. The author points out that physical education is required for children and youth between ages three and twenty-one who qualify for special education because of a specific disability or developmental delay.

The article points out that physical education activities for students with disabilities will have relatively more restrictions and some will be somewhat less vigorous, depending on the individual needs of the student. The physical education teacher, in collaboration with the school principal and support staff, decides on the vigorousness of program activities and the adaptation of equipment and support required to meet the needs of the student with disabilities. For example, partner assistance, along with larger baseball bats and balls or lower basketball hoops, may be called for. The student's IEP will provide some information regarding physical exercise, including specific considerations for different body parts, protective equipment, endurance and rest periods, and so forth.

When students with disabilities are included in physical education classes with students without disabilities, the instructor must give consideration to how an activity might be adapted to meet the needs of all students. Yoga has been shown to work especially well in adaptive settings. Personal assistance from a teacher's aide or qualified parent volunteer has proven most beneficial. Other strategies include creating new physical-education tasks in which the disabled student can be successful. To avoid the handicapped student always being the last one selected for teams or group activities, it seems wise to on occasion allow the student to serve as "captain" and be the one to select team members.

Snapshot 6: The staff member student advocate and the homeless and failing fifth-grade student who really wanted to know.

A homeless child is disabled in the sense that he or she is truly disadvantaged. Homeless children commonly live in automobiles, on the street, in city parks, or in other dismal surroundings. The comforts of a home with all the modern conveniences are foreign to most homeless children.

One homeless boy was not doing well in school academically and his family life was just as you would expect. On one occasion, the school had a special program related to survival methods in the wilderness and invited a "mountain man" to tell about his experiences in the woods. At one point, the homeless boy raised his hand and asked, "What do you use to wipe your butt?" The teachers and others in attendance were appalled and wanted the boy removed from the room immediately. Some wanted him suspended from school. Only one staff member and the school principal understood that the homeless boy really wanted to know the answer to his question. He faced this problem in his life every day. In spite of the skepticism of many, with the support of the principal the staff member took the opportunity to engage with the boy's interest in survival strategies by linking his studies with it. Reading, writing, and math lessons were tied to survival strategies. The boy was offered a focus on something that he really cared about and so was helped on the road to academic improvement and a new interest in learning. The courage of the staff member in standing up for the student should not be overlooked. Advocating for students in unpopular circumstances requires a great deal of courage. The advocate support of the school principal was crucial in this case.

Snapshot 7: The principal's weekend ride that led to his understanding.

Mr. Smith was in his second year as principal of College View Middle School. CV Middle School enrolled a diverse student population, with 25 percent of the students coming from Bluemont, the lower-income area of the school district. Fifty percent of the middle-school students lived in the middle-income area of the district, and the remaining 25 percent were bused in from a military base located outside the district.

Kenny was an eighth-grade student who was considered by three of his subject-matter teachers as a borderline special-education student. He lived in the Bluemont area and rode the school bus to and from school each day. Kenney's achievement test scores were below grade level. His low grades were due partially to the fact that he seldom if ever completed the daily homework assignments. Teachers were reluctant to keep him after school to do homework because he would have to miss his ride home on the bus. He had been sent to the school nurse on several occasions for what was termed "lack of personal grooming." Whether to retain Kenny in grade 8 or place him in the special-education program had been given much thought. One weekend, Principal Smith and his wife decided to drive through Bluemont, just to become more familiar with the environment. As they were driving up a dirt road they noticed several children playing in the ditch near the road-side. One looked up and hollered, "Hello Mr. Smith." It was Kenney, who recognized his principal from his several visits to his office. Mr. Smith did wave to Kenny but drove on down the road. Principal and Mrs. Smith noticed several things about the house in which Kenney apparently lived. There were no visible electrical lines into the house. There was an outhouse on the property and apparently no modern plumbing inside. One old-fashioned water hand pump was seen at the side of the house. Principal Smith thought about what he had seen throughout the weekend. It was no wonder that Kenny had problems doing his homework under such conditions. He wondered, given the circumstances, how Kenney was able to come to school each day as well groomed as he did. He asked himself how many other CV students lived in similar difficult conditions. The following Tuesday was the biweekly faculty meeting. Principal Smith announced the establishment of the "homework service room" that would be available to any student after school for forty-five minutes each day. A notice of this provision was sent to all parents, who were alerted also that their child would be home later than usual on days when they used the homework service room. A special feature was noted: "Refreshments will be served."

Who was to monitor the homework service room? Principal Smith appointed himself to the role with the announcement that "the homework service room will be a priority for me." On occasion, volunteer teachers, selected students, and volunteer parents would be available to help students with homework. Special-education students were common among the many students who took advantage of the new school services.

But what about the bus schedule problems? School bus schedules would serve the needs of the students. Later in the program, district schools were able to hire qualified teacher aides to help with the special homework services. In addition, Principal Smith's concerns led to increased services by the social-work division of the school district. Kenny and other students did not always complete all of their homework in the service room. However, the successful start given to them in the service room motivated them to more frequently complete their work at home. In addition, classroom teachers were encouraged to give some time in class each day to initiate homework assignments. When the school's teachers began to notice the academic improvement in students who participated in the homework sessions, many volunteered their services as well. Yes, Kenney's school performance improved considerably. By the end of the school year there was no more talk about retaining him in grade.

Snapshot 8: The school principal uses a systems approach as a model for student advocacy.

The second-grade student was unmanageable and could not stay in a regular classroom situation for any period of time without causing a major disturbance. He was reading one year below grade level. The student was emotionally disturbed and would leave the school campus without notice every chance he had. The problems were compounded by the fact that the student's mother was unsupportive of the son and of the school personnel.

The principal initiated her advocacy for the student by soliciting the support of the special-education personnel in the school and the district and of the classroom teachers. The principal's position was that to be a student advocate the principal must also be a teacher advocate. Ultimately, the principal, regular classroom teachers, special-education teachers, the school counselor, and the student's parents collaborated to monitor the student's daily school activities. This "several persons" scheme served as a systems approach for tying the needs of the student to the expertise of the several team members. The team met continuously to deliberate on the status of the student and to delegate training needs relative to who does what. The team's initial success with the student began to build-in additional support from others on the staff.

Teachers became knowledgeable of the student's needs and interests and used this information to motivate him toward meaningful learning activities. The teachers required deliberate effort from the student but were compassionate in their relationships with him. The student's progress was monitored continuously and his placement was altered accordingly. (The principal thus gained a better knowledge of the staff's capabilities and their compassion levels, and he used this information for more successful program placements generally.)

At the time of this writing, the student was in grade 4 and able to remain in the regular classroom with his peers for one-half of his school time. In grade 2, his average time in the regular classroom had been only one hour each day. In grade 2, he had been reading one year below grade level. In grade 4 he is reading two grades above grade level.

This snapshot underscores the following imperatives for the principal student advocate:

♦ Build a strong support team for the disabled student.
♦ Be not only a student but a teacher advocate as well.
♦ Use a system's approach to advocacy, with a range of expertise on the team.

- ◆ Know staff capabilities, as the knowledge aids the important functions of support and student placement.
- ◆ Be courageous and bold in your advocacy for programs and policies that benefit students with disabilities.

Snapshot 9: The case of the advocate principal and the belligerent young lady.

Amelia was a sixth-grade student with cerebral palsy (CP) and disabilities in language and speech. English was not her first language. Amelia failed to attend school regularly, had difficulty dealing with peers and adults, had no social skills, was a consummate liar, and as the principal noted, could cuss in two languages.

As is common, Amelia disliked others knowing about her disabilities. She would do anything possible to "cover up" her physical and language problems. The principal stated that Amelia was "dumb-smart," meaning that she was street smart and could play the game and act out a part depending on the occasion.

The principal was in his fifth year as school leader and indicated that he had made it clear at the outset of his tenure that he favored inclusion. The problem was that no teacher wanted Amelia in class, and even the special-education teachers did not want her in the school. In spite of these feelings, the principal kept Amelia in the school. He worked with the staff and encouraged them to set aside their predispositions and find ways to help in her communication, in needed adjustments in homework arrangements, in gaining her trust, and in equitable treatment flexible assessment. Every effort was made to help Amelia feel "normal." She refused to be treated differently and continued to refuse help from others when she fell down or needed other physical support.

In some matters, the principal and team members needed to use forced involvement on a consistent and ongoing basis. In others, isolation was needed. Slowly, trust began to develop between the professional staff and Amelia. Both her academic skills and her social skills had improved significantly by grade 8. The school principal helped Amelia build connections and establish relationships, and after two years she is doing well in an inclusive classroom setting.

(Postscript: Toward the end of the interview with the school principal, he asked the interviewer if he would like to meet Amelia. Of course, the interviewer said that he would be delighted to do so. The principal asked the secretary to call Amelia to the office. Upon her entrance into the office, the principal made it clear to her that, she wasn't in any trouble but that a visitor wanted to meet her since she was doing so well in school. The interviewer asked Amelia about her favorite things to do and she was hesitant to respond. He asked if she had a favorite subject and she shook her head no. The principal asked her what she did to have fun and Amelia said she played with her dog. He asked if she liked the computers and then she began to open up. "Yes, I like the computers," she said. She commented that she liked to write. The interviewer responded that he also liked to write and that she might find writing as one of her several talents. As she was getting ready to return to class the principal picked up the student's backpack and said, "This is heavy, what in the world do you have in here?" She smiled and said, "I have rocks in there." Of course, that was one of Amelia's jokes.)

Snapshot 10: The dedicated principal student advocate supports a learning disabled/gifted student.

Rex had a discrepant pattern of abilities that included severe learning disabilities in reading, writing, and spelling and superior abilities in mathematics and science. In the early elementary school years, teachers, counselors, and others had been somewhat confused about Rex's condition, since he was able to achieve satisfactorily in school and also was able to "cover up" his disabilities through such behaviors as noninvolvement in classroom discussions while giving the appearance of involvement in small group activities when the goal was a group project. Rex's deficits included poor memory skills and difficulty with visual-motor integration and visual/auditory processing. These deficits were accompanied by feelings of low self-respect. He was sent to the school principal's office often for disciplinary reasons. After completing grade 4, he was diagnosed as a learning disabled/gifted student, through standardized and academic tests identifying strengths and weaknesses.

After learning of Rex's diagnosis, the school principal gave considerable thought to the proper placement for him. After conferences with the school counselor, classroom teachers, and special-education personnel, Rex's placement was changed to include more individualization in classes with other gifted peers and in classes with teachers who understood Rex's weaknesses and strengths and adjusted lessons accordingly. By grade 6, Rex had become a different student. Although remedial instruction was continued in some areas, instructional emphasis was placed on his strengths. Special attention was given to his special interests, using appropriate instructional and motivational aids. The advocate team, chaired by the school principal, programmed opportunities for the student to excel. The team agreed that such programmed opportunities, planned individualization, a focus on the student's gifts, and positive feedback from the principal, teachers, and others concerning his performance all served to motivate Rex's academic and behavioral improvements. His self-esteem and peer relationships were also improved.

Snapshot 11: A long-term advocacy with a positive ending for a student with bipolar disorder.

Bipolar disorder is a lifelong disability that commonly affects how one feels and how one acts. Bipolar disorder, also referred to as manic-depressive disorder and mood disorder, can cause extreme swings from manic highs to depressive lows. A first-grade student with a bipolar disorder had the entire school staff at its wits' end. At this point in her life, Ruth was not assessed as qualified for special education. Experienced teachers in the school, the school counselor, and others had nearly given up on her case; the counselor indicated that she had used all the skills that she had without success. Since Ruth was not in special education, the staff was fearful of giving the needed support. Ruth's "meltdowns" were characterized by acts of rage. For example, she might be coloring and without any known reason start screaming, breaking and throwing the crayons, and kicking the surrounding tables and chairs.

The school principal called on a reading teacher to see what she could do to help Ruth in the early grades. Upon receiving a call that Ruth was having one of her meltdowns, the reading teacher would appear and take Ruth to her office. In the office, Ruth would continue to scream, kick things, and be belligerent during the teacher's efforts to calm her down. Ruth's therapy at this point consisted primarily of spending time with this teacher and talking to her about how she felt. When Ruth entered first grade, a study of the family history suggested to school personnel that her bipolar disorder had been inherited. The principal and reading teacher spent time with the family and assisted them in gaining accessing the various community resources that would give them and Ruth some support.

School personnel continued to monitor Ruth's behavior. Her meltdowns were not always set off by an external event; they just happened. Ruth had informed the teacher advocate that she could tell when one of her meltdowns was about to occur and that she needed an outlet. She would scream, kick, and throw things because, as she said, it made her feel better. Still at this point, the advocate team was at a loss as to what to do. However, they advocated by making themselves available to sit with Ruth and try to calm her down until the rage was over.

By grade 3, the team had taken a more thoughtful and organized approach, which it was hoped would be helpful to Ruth:

- ◆ The team set up observation schedules and arranged for continuous team dialogue.
- ◆ The team continually adjusted Ruth's schedule in order to place her in the most advantageous environment, with a teacher who understood her ongoing problems.
- ◆ The team arranged for more personal choices for Ruth, keeping, however, the range of choices within the control of the team.
- ◆ The team became much better at predicting Ruth's meltdowns and encouraged her not to wait to tell the staff when she felt that one was oncoming. When a problem appeared to be coming, a team advocate was radioed to come to the site to help.
- ◆ The team continued to use the strategy of escape when it was needed, in order to remove Ruth to a safe place before she could hurt herself or others. Her rage instances tended to be less destructive and more controlled as time went on.
- ◆ A therapy of talking to Ruth and attempting to move her away from danger was initiated.

The school principal and reading advocate emphasize that the right team members are of paramount importance in such cases. Here, the school counselor tended to add to the Ruth's problems rather than advocate for resolving them. Although the reading teacher moved to another school and then to a position in the district's central office, she continued to follow the case and support the advocate team whenever she was called upon to do so.

At the time of this writing, Ruth was a successful high school student. Her special needs were continuously monitored and her educational settings altered accordingly. She had been successful in self-contained special-education classes and in classes with her grade-level peers. In the interview, the school advocate reported that Ruth had no problems regarding her academics at this time. The advocate made one highly significant point as the interview ended. She stated, "Any school principal can become an advocate for special-education students by connecting to the many available and valuable resources."

Bipolar disorder often changes for the better or for the worse at puberty. There is now medication that is helpful in controlling the behavioral swings. However, in too many instances the disabled individual stops taking the medication when things improve, in which case the problems usually reoccur.

Snapshot 12: The principal advocate helps a language disabled child by gaining support of the family.

Jimmy was five years old and enrolled in kindergarten. He had severe speech/language disabilities that were accompanied by behavior problems. Since he could not communicate clearly through speech, he would attempt to gain the attention of others by grabbing and shaking them, standing up and walking around the room at inappropriate times, and being otherwise physically disruptive in order to gain attention.

Jimmy's parents were aware that his speech was a problem and that his behavior was not normal. However, they believed that these were matters of his age and that eventually he would grow out of them. Jimmy's disabilities were unattended to at home. Upon his entrance to kindergarten, he was unable to take turns in any activity, raise his hand to participate, or comply with any of the classroom procedures. When he had to relieve himself, he would pull down his pants and attempt to do so. After all, this is what he did at home.

The school staff members were of the opinion that the child should be withheld from kindergarten for at least another year. He could not be understood and was extremely disruptive in class. However, the school principal was of the opinion that this child could be helped and supported his continuation in kindergarten. It was obvious to the principal that to be successful in school Jimmy had to have the support of his family at home. Jimmy's parents were working against the child's progress by allowing him to do whatever he wanted at home. Although all of the school's personnel became aware of Jimmy's problems, at first one classroom teacher was primarily in charge of learning program. At the outset, the teacher felt somewhat isolated. The school principal became her primary support, by clarifying Jimmy's needs and working with the teacher on being more inclusive. Then a team consisting of the school principal, the classroom teacher, the special-education teacher, the speech instructor, the counselor, and a cafeteria representative was organized to advocate for Jimmy. Rather than sending Jimmy home or isolating him, a plan was devised to attempt to help resolve Jimmy's disabilities, a positive behavior plan for implementation in school and at home.

The school had access to a speech specialist two days per week. However, the speech teacher worked with the classroom teacher and others so that they could reinforce the child's speech lessons in on other days. The school's special-education teacher spent time in the regular classroom to support the efforts of that teacher. The goal was to increase the child's success in the classroom.

Even at this young age, the child loved the computer. The positive behavior plan included Jimmy earning computer time by improving his ability to follow directions, keeping his pants on, raising his hand, and keeping his hands off of other children. His parents were apprised of the procedures to be used at home for helping Jimmy improve and of the outside resources that should be used to support his development. Jimmy's family began to reinforce the team's messages concerning proper methods of communication, dress and bathroom habits, listening, and adherence to directions. For example, the computer-use award for good behavior and speech improvement therapy were practiced at home as well. The chaos at home was lessened.

After a relative short time period, the consistency of the school-family positive behavior plan resulted in Jimmy's ability to remain in the regular classroom for a half day. After only eight weeks, the large majority of the school staff was saying, "our positive behavior plan is working." The child's success in learning was beginning to emerge.

The Student Advocacy Traits Post-Test

Since this is our final chapter, we recommend that you retake the Student Advocacy Traits assessment in Chapter 1 and check your results. Did you raise your SAT score one level or perhaps two? If so, give yourself a pat on the back; your student advocacy traits are growing.

Summary

This chapter has focused on principal student advocates and their work in the special-education programs. Considerable progress in serving students with disabilities has been made since the early 1960s, and today approximately six million disabled students are being served in public schools in the United States.

A brief review of special-education programs and requirements was presented and the common responsibilities of the school principal in special education were described. A true/false quiz was included for checking your knowledge of the legal requirements for special-education programs and activities.

The primary laws and regulations that guide special education and its provisions in schools were discussed with emphasis given to Section 504 of the Rehabilitation Act of 1973, the Education for All Handicapped Children

Act of 1975, and the Individuals with Disabilities Education Act of 1990. The provisions of these federal laws and their related amendments set forth the required provisions for all children with disabilities for schools that receive federal funding for special-education programs.

How do principal student advocates serve students with disabilities? How do you know a principal student advocate when you see one? Student advocates provide for relevant professional development for all teachers, hold high expectations for students with disabilities, encourage interventions that promote opportunities for student learning, and focus on positive outcomes for all students with disabilities. Principal student advocates are recognized by the commitments they make to the goals and objectives of special education, by where they spend their time, by how they choose to act and make their actions known concerning special education programs and activities, by how they organize the staff and their physical surroundings, and by the personal courage they display in their support of students with disabilities by standing up for student rights and working to change laws and policies that are not in the best interests of student with disabilities.

Competency-based administration and its importance to the work of the school principal was discussed in relation to the primary tasks, competencies, and indicators of competency relevant to successful leadership in special-education administration.

Several school principals, special-education directors, and teachers were interviewed, with a focus on their student advocacy experiences in special-education programs. "Snapshots" of their experiences were given.

Application Exercises

1. Resolved: "School principals have not been sufficiently prepared to assume the primary leadership for the special-education program in their schools. Therefore, special-education programs and services should be delegated to the special-education personnel in the school and supervised by the central office of the school district."

Take the pro or con side of this resolution and write the primary points that you would present in a debate. Avoid weakening your argument with such equivocations as "it all depends" or "both should cooperatively assume leadership responsibility." The question is, "Should the school principal be the person responsible for leading the implementation and evaluation of the special-education program and services in his or her school?"

2. Go back to the section "**Select Special-Education Competencies of School Principals**" in this chapter and select one of the seventeen listed

competencies. Then develop a minimum of five indicators of competency appropriate to it. Keep in mind that indicators are overt behaviors that show that the skill is being practiced.

3. Examine your work calendar for a recent week. Think about the meetings, telephone calls, observations, student contacts, parental conversations, decisions, and program activities it shows. How many of these events involved the special-education program or students with disabilities? Consider your particular involvement and the outcomes of each of these events. Which, if any, revealed your personal behaviors as a principal student advocate? Be prepared to pat yourself on the back.

4. Give some thought to the many classroom subjects taught by teachers in your school. Then review Snapshot 5 (page 111). Select one of the subjects (e.g., reading, science, art, etc.) being taught. What changes in the program determinants might be appropriate to the subject selected for more effective accommodation of students with disabilities (see page 15)?

References

American Youth Policy Forum and Center on Education Policy. (2002). *Twenty-five years of educating children with disabilities.* Washington, DC: American Youth Policy Forum and Center on Education Policy.

Bennis, W. (1989). *On becoming a leader.* Reading, MA: Addison-Wesley.

Broughton, E. (2005). *Minimizing conflict, maximizing collaboration.* http://www .principals partnership.com/dec05feature.doc

Burrello, L. C., & Lashley, C. A. (1992). *Educating all students together: How school leaders create unified systems.* Thousand Oaks, CA: Corwin Press–Sage.

Bush, G. W. (1999). *A charge to keep.* NY: William Morrow.

Churchill, W. (1940). *Speech given to the House of Commons of the Parliament of the United Kingdom* (June 4). Guardian.co.uk

Container Store, The. *What we stand for: Our foundation principles.* http://standfor .containerstore.com/our-foundation-principles/

Cooner, D., Tocherman, S., & Garrison-Wade, D. (2005-2006). Preparing principals for leadership in special education: Applying ISLLC standards. *Journal of Principal Preparation and Development, 6,* 19–24.

Denton, P. (2007). *The power of our words: Teacher language that helps children learn.* Turners Falls, MA: Foundation for Children.

Evans, J. H., Bird, K. M., Ford, I. A., Green, J. L., & Bischoff, R. A. (1992). Strategies for overcoming resistance to the integration of students with special needs into neighborhood schools: A case study. *CASE in Point, 7,* 1–15.

Guzman, N. (1997). Leadership for successful inclusive schools: A study of principal behaviors. *Journal of Educational Administration, 35* (5), 439–450.

Guzman, N., & Schofield, R. (1995). *Systematic restructuring for successful inclusive schools: Leadership and a collaborative evaluation model.* Paper presented at the annual meeting of the American Association of School Administrators (AASA).

Haberman, M. (1995). *Star teachers of children in poverty.* Bloomington, IN: Kappa Delta Pi.

Hargrove, R. (1998). *Mastering the art of creative collaboration.* New York: Business Week Books, McGraw Hill.

Higley Unified School District. (2010). *Code of conduct 2010-2011.* Higley, AZ.

Huszczo, G. E. (1996). *Tools for team excellence.* Mountain View, CA: Davies-Black Publishing.

International Center for Leadership in Education. (2010). *Rigor/relevance framework.* Retrieved November 26, 2010, from http://www.leadered.com/pdf/ R&Rframework.pdf

Jobs, S. Steve Jobs Apple. *YouTube.* http://www.youtube.com/watch?v= qjxacrSCYRE&feature=player_embedded

Jones, P., & Kahaner, L. (1995). *Say it and live it: The 50 corporate mission statements that hit the mark.* NY: Currency Doubleday.

Lavoie, R. (2008). *Fighting the good fight: How to advocate for your students without losing your job.* Washington, D. C.: LD OnLine. http://www.ldonline.org/

Lezotte, L. (2002). *Assembly required: A continuous school improvement system.* Okenos, MI: Effective School Products.

Lezotte, L. & McKee-Snyder, K. (2011). *What effective schools do.* Bloomington, IN: Solution Tree Press.

Lombardi, V. (2010). *Vince Lombardi: Quotes.* http://www.vincelombardi.com/quotes.html

Loyola University Maryland. *About Loyola: Mission, values, and vision.* http://www.loyola.edu/about.aspx

Manus, B. (1992). *Visionary leadership: Creating a compelling sense of direction for your organization.* San Francisco, CA: Jossey-Bass.

Maslow, A. H. (1987). *Motivation and personality* (3rd ed). New York: Harper Collins. First published 1954.

McAnely, F. X. (1992). *The impact of school principals' attitudes toward mainstreaming on student referrals.* PhD dissertation, Temple University. Dissertation Abstracts International, *53*(10A), 3495.

Norton, M. S. (2008). *Human resources administration for educational leaders.* Thousand Oaks, CA: Sage.

Norton, M. S., Hartwell-Hunnicutt, K., & Norton, R. C. (1996). The learning disabled-gifted student. *Contemporary Education, 68* (1), 36–40.

Phi Delta Kappa. (1973). *School climate improvement: A challenge to the school administrator.* Bloomington, IN: Phi Delta Kappa.

Porras, J., Emery, S., & Thompson, M. (2007). *Success built to last: Creating a life that matters.* Upper Saddle River, NJ: Wharton School Publishing.

Praisner, C. L. (2003). Attitudes of elementary school principals toward inclusion of students with disabilities. *Exceptional Children, 69* (2), 135–145.

Princeton Review, The. (2010). *Guidance Counselor.* Retrieved November 26, 2010, from http://www.princetonreview.com/Careers.aspx?cid=75

Ravitch, D. (1985). *The troubled crusade: American education, 1945–1980.* New York: Basic Books.

Support for Texas Academic Renewal. (1997). *Successful texas schoolwide programs: Research study results.* Austin, TX: Charles A Dana Center, University of Texas.

Ulrich, D., Zenger, J., & Smallwood, N. (1999). *Results based leadership: How leaders build the business and improve the bottom line.* Boston, MA: Harvard Business School Press.

US Department of Education, National Center for Education Statistics. (2010). *Digest of Education Statistics* (NCES 2010-013). Table 180 and Chapter 2.

Watson, S. (2008). *How to integrate special needs students into physical education.* About.com: Special Education. http://specialed.about.com/od/teacherstrategies/a/phe.htm

Zenter, J. H., Musselwhite, E., Hurson, K., & Perrin, C. (1994). *Leading teams: mastering the new role.* Burr Ridge, IL: Irwin Professional Publishing.